＊Each recipe is 4 servings unless otherwise indicated.

MUSHROOMS

HERBS and SPICES

LIGHT-COLORED VEGETABLES

ROOT VEGETABLES

SEA VEGETABLES

Why Do We Eat Vegetables?

— Eat with a relish —

Eating Unwillingly Causes Opposite Effect

We used to eat food without any particular purpose, just because it was tasty or popular. Recently, however, there is a tendency to choose foods with health and nourishment in mind. Since vegetables are rich in a variety of nourishment, they have recently come to attract public attention as an edible medicine.

It is not advisable, however, to try to eat tasteless vegetables reluctantly just for their effects. It will become a cause of stress, and eventually of illness. In some cases, nutritious vegetables bring out bad effects.

Weight Loss and Prevention of Colon Cancer

Lack of vegetables in the diet results in weight gain. Vegetables contain a large quantity of water and fibers, which satiate the appetite while passing through the digestive organs without producing energy. Moreover, the vegetable fibers help the bowels keep active and relieve constipation, thus aiding weight loss.

Relief from constipation keeps the bowels in good condition. Excessive fat and cholesterol are discharged and colon cancer is prevented. The recent increase in colon cancer comes from the insufficient intake of vegetables.

By Asako Tohata, M.D.

Eat Brightly Green and Yellow Vegetables

The most recommended vegetables are colored ones such as spinach, broccoli, and carrots, which contain a lot of vitamins A and C.

Vitamin A strengthens skin and mucous membranes, and it is good for eyes and for the prevention of colds.

Vitamin C is effective in relieving stress and a must for cold prevention and an energetic life. Since it is related with collagen, the main component of bones, it is an indispensable nutrient for teeth and bones. It is also useful for the prevention of cataracts. Vitamins A and C are known as cancer preventive. Of course, you should eat lots of other vegetables which are full of vitamin C and minerals.

How to Eat with Relish

Vegetables with bitter flavor tend to ruin the taste and disturb the absorption of iron, but these problems disappear if the harshness is removed. What is important is to work out a new idea as to how to eat those vegetables with relish. Eating with pleasure is the most effective way.

DR. TOHATA is a prominent personality in Japan. Specializing in diet and nutrition, she lectures, writes, and appears on TV. She has spoken for many years at Ochanomizu University and Kagawa Nutrition College in Tokyo, and she has written 50 books in Japanese. Dr. Tohata holds a Doctor of Medicine from Toho University.

Eat more

How to Intake Nutrients

Nutrients Contained in Vegetables

Vitamin A (daily requirement: men 2,000 I.U., women 1,800 I.U.)

Vitamin A helps maintain healthy skin and mucous membranes, and promotes good vision in dim light. It is also said to be effective against cancer. Since it is fat-soluble, children should be careful not to take an excessive amount. Vitamin A deficiency inhibits bodily growth, the development of teeth and skeletal tissue, causes night blindness and inflammation of the eyes. Skin and mucous membranes harden and become cracked. Vitamin A is contained in carrots and green leafy vegetables. (See below)

Vitamin B_1 (daily requirement: adult men 0.8〜1.0 mg, adult women 0.7〜0.8 mg)

As vitamin B_1 is water-soluble, it is not stored in the body. It helps cells convert carbohydrates into energy and prevent obesity. A deficiency can cause fatigue, drowsiness, beriberi, nerve damage, constipation, edema and heart trouble. Vitamin B_1 is contained in beans and sesame seeds.

Vitamin B_2 (daily requirement: adult men 1.2〜1.4 mg, adult women 1.0〜1.1 mg)

Vitamin B_2 plays an essential role in the metabolism of amino acids, fats and carbohydrates. A deficiency can cause inflammation of the lips and cornea, and makes the eyes sensitive to bright light. Leading sources are liver, cheese, and fermented soybeans. It is also found in mushrooms.

Vitamin C (daily requirement: adult 50 mg)

About 1.5 grams of vitamin C are stored in the body. It helps promote healthy gums and teeth. It produces collagen, maintaining normal connective tissue. It strengthens blood vessels and cartilage and increases resistance to colds. A deficiency can cause scurvy, subcutaneous bleeding, anemia and insufficient growth of bones. Outstanding sources are strawberries, citrus fruits, broccoli and green leafy vegetables.

Vitamin D (daily requirement: adult 100 I.U.)

Vitamin D may be obtained from dietary sources, but it is also manufactured by the body after exposure to sunshine, and stored mainly in the

Vegetables containing vitamin A (I.U./100 g)		
1	Amanori laver (dried) *	14,000
2	Aonori laver *	12,000
3	Dried red chili pepper *	11,000
4	Shiso (perilla) leaf**	4,800
5	Parsley**	4,200
6	Carrot	4,100
7	Malabar nightshade	2,000
8	Garland chrysanthemum	1,900
9	Komatsuna	1,800
9	Chinese chive	1,800

Vegetables containing vitamin C (mg/100 g)		
1	Parsley**	200
2	Broccoli	160
3	Brussels sprouts	150
4	Rape blossoms	120
5	Amanori laver(dried)**	100
6	Sweet pepper	90
7	Sweet pepper leaves	85
8	Pepper	80
8	Malabar nightshade	80
10	Komatsuna	75

Vegetables containing dietary fiber (g/10 g)		
1	Agar-agar *	8.13
2	Cloud ear mushroom *	7.42
3	Hijiki seaweed	5.49
4	Dried shiitake mushroom**	4.34
5	Aonori laver *	3.86
6	Wakame seaweed	3.80
7	Amanori laver (dried)	2.97
8	Kombu seaweed	2.86
9	Kidney beans	1.98
10	Adzuki beans	1.60

*Eat 2 grams at a time. **Eat 5〜10 grams at a time.

Effectively from Vegetables

liver. It helps form and maintain healthy skin and tissue, promoting the absorption of calcium, which is necessary for the develpment of bones. It is also said to have anticancer effect. Megadoses can be toxic and dangerous, since it is stored in the body. A deficiency leads to soft bones, rickets, and osteoporosis. Cloud ears (Kikurage mushrooms) and dried shiitake mushrooms contain vitamin D.

Vitamin E (daily requirement: adult men 8 mg, adult women 7 mg)

Vitamin E protects vitamin A and fats against the damage of oxidation, and helps form red blood cells. This vitamin is indispensable for normal pregnancy. A deficiency makes a person unable to walk and spatial judgement. Germs of cereals, nuts and green leafy vegetablcs are rich in vitamin E.

Calcium (daily requirement: adult 0.6 g)

Calcium is largely responsible for the hardness of bones and teeth and helps the blood coagulate during bleeding. It is also necessary for the proper functions of enzyme. A deficiency results in weak bones and teeth and makes a person highly nervous. Main sources are small fish, sesame seeds, and seaweed.

Iron (daily requirement: adult men 10 mg, adult women 12 mg)

Iron is essential to the formation of hemoglobin, which carries oxygen in the blood. It also helps the cells obtain energy from food. A deficiency leads to fatigue, forgetfullness and anemia. Hijiki (edible brown algae) and parsley are rich in iron.

Dietary fiber (daily requirement: adult 20～25 g)

The fiber contained in vegetables and mushrooms is insoluble in water, while the fiber contained in seaweed and fruits are soluble. Dietary fiber helps ease bowel movement and prevent constipation. It also plays a role in reducing cholesterol and protects against the leading chronic diseases, heart disease, cancer, and diabetes.

Preparation and Preservation

Vegetables that contain fat-soluble vitamins like A, D and E should be cooked with oil or oily foods such as sesame seeds or nuts. Vitamins C and B are sensitive to heat and can easily be leached away, so leafy green vegetables should be cooked quickly and immediately chilled in cold water. The loss of vitamin C is accelerated when food is being stored, so vegetables should be properly wrapped and refrigerated. It is important to pay attention to cooking methods and preservation of food to conserve nutrients.

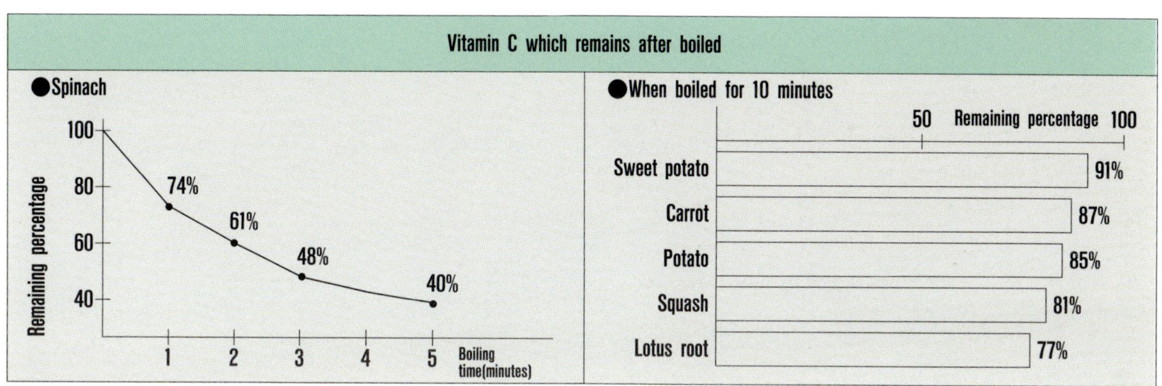

The amount of the dietary fiber on the previous page is based on books published by Ishiyaku Shuppan (1986) and vitamins by a book published by Joshi Eiyo Daigaku (1991).

GREEN and YELLOW VEGETABLES

When thinking of green and yellow vegetables, spinach and carrots come to mind. Both vegetables contain beta carotene and green vegetables are full of vitamin C. Vitamin A is essential for skin and eyes and vitamin C is effective in preventing stress. Green and yellow vegetables are most highly recommended among vegetable varieties.

GREEN ASPARAGUS

For prevention of adult diseases and constipation

Asparagus is full of glucide, vitamins A, C, B_2, as well as dietary fiber. It contains rutin, which protects blood vessels and reduces blood pressure, and plenty of aspartic acid, which activates metabolism and relieves fatigue. It is also said to increase the discharge of urine.

Effective for
Preventing hypertension
Relieving fatigue
Diuretic

Plenty of Vitamins A and C

Green Asparagus Quiche

Ingredients: 16 stalks asparagus / salt / egg mixture (4 eggs / 2 cups milk / 8 Tbsps grated cheese / salt and pepper) / paprika / butter

Method: 1. Cut off tough stem ends and boil in salted water, then cut into 1 inch (3 cm) lengths.

2. Break eggs into a bowl and mix well with milk, cheese, salt and pepper.

3. Place the asparagus on a slightly buttered oven proof dish. Cover with the egg mixture. (see photo)

4. Preheat oven to 320°F (160°C). Place dish in a pan of hot water and then bake uncovered for 15 to 20 minutes until slightly browned.

5. Sprinkle with paprika.

* Boil asparagus for only a short time so that it retains vitamin C and its crispy texture.

Japanese-style dish with bonito flakes

Fried Asparagus Seasoned with Dried Bonito Flakes

Ingredients: 24 stalks slim green asparagus / 4 Tbsps sesame oil / 2½ Tbsps sake / 2½ Tbsps happo dashi (see inside front cover) / 1 cup dried bonito flakes

Method: 1. Cut off tough stem ends and cut into 2 inch (5 cm) lengths.

2. Heat sesame oil in a pan and stir-fry asparagus quickly.

3. Pour sake and dashi over them. Boil down until the soup thickens.

4. Serve on a plate. Sprinkle with dried bonito flakes.

* Add dried bonito flakes just before turning off the heat, then stir quickly and serve.

Cream of Asparagus

Ingredients and method: 1. Peel 8 stalks asparagus with a knife and boil in salted water until very tender and cut into ¼ inch (1cm) lengths. Slice ½ small onion. Cut 2 potatoes in half, then into slices.

2. Sauté the onion with 1 Tbsp butter in a pan and add the potato. Cover with water and cook for 15 minutes. Put asparagus in the pan and continue to cook for another 10 minutes. Put contents in an electric blender.

3. Heat the mixture in a pan. Add ½ cup heavy cream and salt and pepper to taste, stirring occasionally until hot, but not boiling. Ladle into bowls. Garnish with asparagus tips and sprinkle with corn flakes.

BROCCOLI

The content of vitamin C is 3.5 times as much as that of a lemon / Indispensable for stress reduction

Effective for

Preventing colds

Intestinal regulation

Preventing anemia

Broccoli contains vitamin A as well as vitamin C, and strengthens the mucous membranes of the throat, nose and stomach. It is also rich in iron and calcium and prevents anemia and osteoporosis. For storage, boil and wrap in plastic wrap and keep in the refrigerator. Be careful not to boil too long or it will lose vitamin C.

Increase calcium with milk / Vegetable cooking rich in iron

Broccoli in White Sauce

Ingredients: 1 large head broccoli (12 oz or 350 g) / 8 sea scallops / juice of 1 clove ginger / Salt / 1 cup milk / 2 bouillon cubes / 1 Tbsp sake / salt and sugar / 1 Tbsp cornstarch / 2 Tbsps salad oil

Method: **1.** Break broccoli into small chunks and parboil in salted water and drain. Cut each scallop into half and top with ginger juice over.

2. Heat oil in a pan and sauté broccoli and scallops for a short time. Premix milk, crushed bouillon cubes, sake, salt and sugar and add to broccoli. Cook for 2 minutes. Thicken with cornstarch dissolved in the same amount of water.

With eggs, a source of good quality of protein

Broccoli and Egg Salad

Ingredients: 1 head broccoli (12 oz or 350 g) / 2 eggs / salt / dressing (2 Tbsps salad oil / 1 Tbsp lemon juice / salt and pepper)

Method: 1. Break broccoli in small chunks and parboil in salted water and drain.

2. Separate hard-cooked eggs into whites and yolks and then mince.

3. Blend dressing ingredients well and mix with broccoli. Top with minced egg whites and yolks.

* Hard-cooked eggs: cover with water and boil for 10 to 12 minutes.

Cooking with oil is a good source of vitamin A

Fritter

Ingredients: 1 head broccoli (12 oz or 300 g) / salt / batter (1 cup sifted flour / Dash salt / 1 egg / 2 tsps oil / 5 Tbsps water) / oil for deep-frying

Method: 1. Break broccoli in small chunks and parboil in salted water and drain.

2. Mix egg yolk, water, flour and salt in a bowl. Let sit for a while. Add oil and fold in egg white beaten stiffly with a spatula.

3. Dip in batter and deep-fry in hot oil (340° ~ 350°F/170° ~ 175°C) until puffy but not brown.

Broccoli is a good source of vitamin C

A close relative of cauliflower, broccoli (a member of Brassica genus), contains two times as much protein and calcium as cauliflower. Compared to green leafy vegetables, broccoli has one third the vitamin A content, but 2.5 times the vitamin C. Broccoli with yellowish and opened florets which has been stored a long time has little vitamin C. Eat it while it is fresh, because long storage will result in a loss of vitamin C. If you want to store it for a long time, boil it, wrap it in a plastic bag and keep it in the refrigerator or freezer.

Effective for
Preventing anemia
Preventing colds
Preventing constipation

SPINACH

Spinach is rich in vitamins A and C, and cellulose. The content of vitamin C is twice as much as that of oranges. It also contains iron and folic acid, which are necessary to make blood.

Spinach Salad

Ingredients: 1 bunch fresh spinach / 4 slices bacon / juice of 1 lemon / salt and pepper / 2 tsps salad oil

Method: **1.** Wash spinach. Strip off any coarse stalks and pat dry on paper towels.

2. Cut bacon in strips and fry in a skillet until crispy.

3. Place spinach in a bowl. Add bacon and pour lemon juice over the salad, sprinkle with salt and pepper. Toss well.

* The stalks can be boiled and seasoned with soy sauce.

Effective for
Preventing osteoporosis
Preventing colds
Preventing anemia

CHINESE MUSTARD GREENS (Ch'ing-keng-ts'ai)

Plenty of vitamins A and C and iron. Contains 130 milligrams of calcium in 100 g.

Mixed Rice with Chinese Mustard Greens

Ingredients: 4 small heads Chinese mustard greens / 2 cups rice / 3 Tbsps salted and dried young sardine / 2 tsps toasted white sesame seeds / ⅔ tsp salt / pepper / 3⅔ Tbsps salad oil

Method: **1.** Wash rice. Cook rice with salt, pepper and ⅔ teaspoon of salad oil added.

2. Cut greens into ½ inch (1 cm) lengths. In a pan heat 3 tablespoons of oil and fry, then add young sardines mixing lightly.

3. Mix with cooked rice, and sesame seeds. Serve in individual bowls.

* If the sardine is salty, rinse with hot water over.

Prepare Animal Food with Leafy Green Vegetables

Leafy green vegetables have plenty of calcium and iron, but they are not enough for a day's necessity. To make up the deficiency, cook with cheese, small fish, (which are rich in calcium), liver and eggs, (which are high in iron). The combination of animal food with vegetables is indispensable for a balanced diet. The following is one good example.

Greens and Liver Stir-fried with Ginger

Ingredients and method: **1.** Wash a bunch of vegetable greens thoroughly and drain. Cut into 1 inch (3 cm) lengths. Mince 1 clove ginger.

2. Rinse 7 ounces (200 g) beef liver under running water to

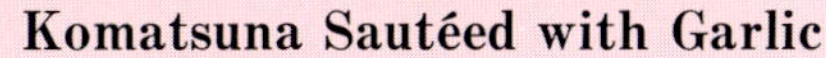

KOMATSUNA
(Brassica rapa)

Contains more vitamins A and C and calcium than spinach. As it is only slightly bitter, little effort is needed to remove the harsh taste.

Effective for
- Preventing colds
- Preventing osteoporosis
- Preventing constipation

Komatsuna Sautéed with Garlic

Ingredients: 1 large bunch komatsuna / 1 big clove garlic / 4 Tbsps dried shrimp / 1 Tbsp sake / ½ tsp salt / 1 tsp soy sauce / 4 Tbsps salad oil

Method: 1. Wash komatsuna in water and drain. Cut into 1½ inch (4 cm) lengths. Separate stalks from leaves.

2. Cut garlic in slices. Soak dried shrimp in water.

3. Heat oil in a skillet and sauté garlic and shrimp until aroma is full. Add stalks of komatsuna and stir-fry.

4. Sauté thoroughly, add leaves of komatsuna and stir-fry. Season with sake, salt and soy sauce.

PAK-CHOI
(Brassica chinensis)

Rich is vitamins A and C. Soft and only slightly bitter. Good for sautéeing with oil and boiling with other ingredients.

Effective for
- Preventing colds
- Preventing anemia
- Preventing constipation

Pak-choi Au Gratin

Ingredients: 2 bunches pak-choi / 2 cups milk / 3 Tbsps flour / 3 Tbsps butter / 2 Tbsps miso (fermented bean paste) / ½ tsps salt / pepper / 1 Tbsp salad oil

Method: 1. Melt butter in a pan and add flour, stirring over low heat carefully not to brown.

2. Add scalded milk and boil until smooth. Add miso and mix well.

3. Cut pak-choi into 4 to 6 pieces and fry in oil. Season with salt and pepper.

4. Place pak-choi in a butterd flame-proof casserole and cover with the aove mixture. Bake in an oven (425°F/220°C) for 10 minutes.

remove blood. Cut into strips and season with each 1⅓ tablespoons of sake and soy sauce. Coat with 2 teaspoons of cornstarch.

3. Heat 2 tablespoons of salad oil in a skillet. Stir-fry ginger and liver then add greens. Season with 2 teaspoons of soy sauce, 2 teaspoons of sake, and a dash of salt. Sprinkle with shichimi-togarashi (a mixture of red pepper and six kinds of spices).

CARROT

Beta carotene and cancer-preventative

Effective for

Preventing colds

Preventing constipation

Eye diseases

Vitamin A is derived from beta carotene, and carrots are the leading source of this substance. One hundred grams of carrots contains 7,300 micrograms of beta carotene. Carotene strengthens the mucous membrane of the throat and eyes and plays an important role in preventing cancer. It is rich in fibers and good for preventing constipation.

The point is to discard the core as it contains little nutritional value or taste

Special Carrot Salad

Ingredients: 9 oz (250 g) carrot (central part discarded) / salt / dressing (1 Tbsp vinegar / 2 Tbsps salad oil / ¼ tsp salt / pepper) / 4 Tbsps raisin / 2 Tbsps of nuts (sliced almonds, peanuts or walnuts)

Method: 1. Slice carrot into julienne strips (2 inches or 5 cm long) and sprinkle with salt. Let stand a few minutes.

2. Wash and drain the water off.

3. Mix with dressing and top with nuts before eating.

For cold prevention

Carrot Potage

Ingredients: 1 carrot (9 oz or 250 g) / 1 small onion / 2/3 cup cooked rice / 2 bouillon cubes / salt and pepper / 4 cups cream / 1 Tbsp butter / 4 Tbsps croutons / minced parsley

Method: 1. Put sliced carrot and onion, cooked rice, 3 cups water, crushed bouillon cubes in a pot and simmer over a moderate heat for about 18 minutes until vegetables are tender.

2. Using an electric blender or food processor blend until smooth.

3. Return all to the pot and season with salt and pepper. Add cream and butter and scald.

4. Sprinkle with parsley and serve with croutons.

Grated Carrot Topping

Ingredients: 1 carrot (9 oz or 250 g) /2 pieces aburaage (deep-fried tofu) / 2 tsps sesame seed oil / juice of 1 clove ginger / 4 Tbsps happo dashi (see inside front cover) / 1 Tbsp mirin (sweet sake)

Method: 1. Grate carrot.

2. Remove excess oil from aburaage by pouring boiling water over it. Chop finely.

3. Put all ingredients in a pan and stir-fry with 5 or 6 chopsticks or a fork. Boil down until the liquid evaporates.

＊ It goes well with rice or noodles.

Drink healthful carrot juice every day

The easiest way of taking vitamin A is to drink carrot juice every day. For those who do not like raw carrot juice, add grated apple or milk. The juice available on the market may be used as the basis for tailor-made drinks. The juice with cellulose content is especially recommended.

[**Carrot Milk**] **Ingredients and method:** Place carrot(3 1/2 oz/100 g) in juicer and make 1/2 cup of carrot juice. Mix well with 1/2 cup milk. Add honey, if desired.

[**Carrot and Apple Juice**]
Ingredients and method: Place carrot (5 1/4 oz/150 g) in juicer and make 3/4 cup of carrot juice. Add 1/4 grated apple and 1 teaspoon lemon. Garnish with mint leaf.

Carrot Milk

Carrot and Apple Juice

PUMPKIN

For clear, smooth skin and cancer prevention

Effective for

Preventing stomach ulcers

Preventing colds

Eye diseases

Besides vitamin A the Western pumpkin contains vitamin C, 39 milligrams in 100 grams, so it is enough to cover the daily requirement of vitamin C (50 milligrams). The Japanese pumpkin is low in nutrients, but it is also low in calories. It strengthens the mucous membranes of the throat, nose, eyes and stomach and is said to prevent cancer.

Plain taste and half the calories of the Western pumpkin

Stuffed Japanese Pumpkin

Ingredients: 1 small Japanese pumpkin (18 oz or 500 g) / 7 oz (200 g) ground beef / 1 onion / 4 fresh shiitake mushrooms / 2 tomatoes / 1 bay leaf / 1 Tbsp curry powder / pepper / ½ Tbsp salad oil / salt / parsley

Method: 1. Cut ⅕ top off pumpkin and remove seeds. Sprinkle with salt inside. Wrap in plastic wrap and cook in microwave oven for 5 minutes.

2. Chop onion and shiitake finely. Pass tomatoes through boiling water and peel. Remove seeds and cut into ⅕ inch (5 mm) cubes.

3. Sauté onion, shiitake, and beef until lightly brown. Add tomato, bay leaf, curry powder, pepper and ¼ teaspoon salt and continue to sauté for another 3 minutes.

4. Stuff pumpkin with (3) and cover with top. Bake in an oven (340~350°F/170~180°C) for 12 to 15 minutes.

Plenty of vitamin C

Pumpkin Meuniere

Ingredients: ¼ pumpkin (14 oz or 400 g) / ¼ tsp salt / pepper / 1 Tbsp flour / 2 tsps salad oil / 2 tsps butter / parsley / lemon

Method: 1. Remove seeds from pumpkin and pare randomly as seen in photo. Cut into ⅕ inch (7 mm) thick arch-shaped slices. Season with salt and pepper and then coat with flour lightly.

2. Heat oil and butter in a skillet and fry each side for 3 minutes until brown.

3. Serve in plate. Sprinkle with parsley and garnish with lemon.

With milk for bones and teeth

Pumpkin Cooked with Milk

Ingredients: ¼ pumpkin (12 oz or 350 g) / 1 cup milk / 1 tsp sugar / 1 tsp butter / ¼ tsp salt / cinnamon

Method: 1. Remove seeds from pumpkin and cut into bite-sized pieces. Pare the skin randomly.

2. Put pumpkin, milk, sugar, salt and butter in a pan and bring to a boil over moderate heat.

3. After boiling, lower heat and simmer for about 10 minutes until tender.

4. Serve in a bowl and sprinkle with cinnamon.

* Do not let milk overflow while cooking. Pare pumpkin randomly to improve the taste and cut corners of pumpkin to keep shape.

Pumpkin seeds are a source of high quality fat

Pumpkin seeds are common ingredients for Chinese cooking like watermelon seeds. They are usually roasted and seasoned with salt. Traditional Chinese medicine uses them as a verumifuge and a tonic. They contain quality protein, fat and vitamin B's and make vegetable dishes tasty and nutritious. The fat is said to be effective in preventing hardening of the arteries. Before roasting the seeds, wash them and dry in the sun. Shell them and season with salt or spices you like.

Expose seeds to the sun for two or three days before roasting.

Effective for
- Relieving fatigue
- Preventing arteriosclerosis
- Preventing hypertension

GREEN PEPPER

Excellent sources of vitamins C and A, and contains rutin, which strengthens capillary vessels

Green Pepper Stuffed with Rice

Ingredients: 8 green peppers / 1½ cups cooked rice / 3 oz (80 g) ground pork / ½ onion / 2 fresh shiitake mushrooms / ½ carrot / salt and pepper / broth (1 cup water / 1 bouillon cube / 1 Tbsp sake / pepper) / 1 Tbsp salad oil / fresh thyme

Method: **1.** Cut off the tops of green pepper as shown in the photo and remove seeds.

2. Mince the vegetables and sauté with ground meat. Season with salt and pepper and mix with rice.

3. Stuff the peppers with (2) and cover. Fasten each cover with a toothpick. Cook in broth for 20 minutes and garnish with thyme.

Effective for
- Increasing stamina
- Relieving fatigue
- Healthy stomach

SCALLION BUDS

Full of vitamins A and C, calcium, potassium and iron. Good for developing physical strength.

Scallion Buds Sautéed with Pork

Ingredients: 9 oz (250 g) scallion buds / 7 oz (200 g) sliced pork / seasoning mixture (2 tsps soy sauce / 2 tsps sake / juice of ½ clove ginger) / 2 tsps cornstarch / salt and pepper / 1 Tbsp salad oil

Method: **1.** Cut pork into ⅛ inch (5 mm) lengths and marinate in seasoning mixture for 20 minutes. Cut scallion buds into 1½ inch (4 cm) lengths.

2. Sprinkle the pork with cornstarch lightly and sauté. Add scallion buds and stir. Season with salt and pepper.

Let's drink more tomato juice

Tomato juice made of fully ripened tomatoes is tasty. Since vitamin C is added, the amount contained in a small can is equivalent to that of 3 raw tomatoes. Make more use of it for cocktails and soups.

[**Tomato Cocktail**] **Ingredients and method:** Mix ⅓ cup of strong black tea with the same amount of tomato juice. Chill in a refrigerator. Garnish with 1 slice of lemon and mint leaves. Add white wine, if you desire.

GARLIC STALKS

See p.41 for its nutrition and effectiveness. The cooking method is simple and you can eat as much as you like.

Effective for
- Relieving fatigue
- Preventing colds
- Improving circulation

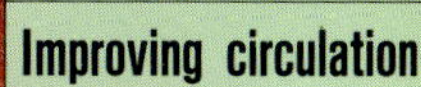

Garlic Stalks Mixed with Sesame Seed Dressing

Ingredients: 16 garlic stalks / 2 oz (50 g) carrot / 2 Tbsps white sesame seeds / 2 tsps soy sauce / 1 tsp sesame seed oil / salt

Method: 1. Boil garlic stalks in salted water and cut into 1 inch (3 cm) lengths.

2. Cut carrot French-style into 1 inch (3 cm) lengths. Boil in salted water. Sprinkle with soy sauce to taste.

3. Toast sesame seeds. Set aside some for topping. Grind the rest of the sesame seeds. Add soy sauce and sesame oil and mix well for dressing.

4. Mix drained vegetables with (3). Sprinkle with the rest of sesame seeds on top.

TOMATO

Contains plenty of vitamin C and rutin, which reduces blood pressure. Select ripened tomatoes.

Effective for
- Preventing hypertension
- Preventing obesity
- Relieving fatigue

Tomato and Mozzarella Cheese

Ingredients: 4 tomatoes / 7 oz (200 g) mozzarella cheese / salt and pepper / 4 Tbsps olive oil / juice of 1 lemon / fresh basil

Method: 1. Peel tomatoes and slice. Sprinkle with salt and pepper.

2. Place tomato slices on a plate and top with mozzarella cheese. Garnish with fresh basil.

3. Pour olive oil and lemon juice over all.

* Mozzarella cheese is a soft, white Italian curd cheese made from water bufflalo milk. It contains a lot of protein and calcium.

[**Spanish-style Tomato Soup**] **Ingredients and method: 1.** Season chilled tomato juice (3 small cans) with salt and pepper. Add minced ½ onion, ½ cucumber, 1 stem parsley and ¼ stalk celery.

2. Mix juice of ½~1 lemon with ½~1 grated lemon peel and 1 Tbsp of olive oil.

3. Serve in bowl with a sliced lemon.

EFFECTIVE GREEN and YELLOW VEGETABLES

Let's try the nutritious cooking of mulukhiya and malabar nightshade. Cooking with green tea is also introduced.

BARILLA

Effective for
Relieving eye fatigue
Preventing colds
Preventing osteoporosis
Relieving stress

Barilla contains as much vitamin A as spinach and about three times as much calcium. It is also an excellent source of vitamin C. Boil and season with soy sauce or dress with other sauces. Fried in batter is also good.

Chinese-style Barilla Salad

Ingredients: 10 oz (300 g) barilla / 1½ oz (40 g) shelled shrimp / 4 dried shiitake mushrooms / 4 ham slices / 1 Tbsp walnuts / salt / 2 tsps sake / 2 tsps soy sauce / (A) (1 Tbsp soy sauce / 1 Tbsp sesame oil / juice of 1 clove ginger / dash salt)

Method: **1.** Boil barilla in salted water and then place in cold water. Cut into bite-sized lengths and drain.

2. Devein shrimp and parch in a pan without using oil. Toast walnuts. Chop shrimp and walnuts coarsely.

3. Soak dried shiitake in ¼ cup warm water. Cook shiitake in the liquid with sake and soy sauce. Cut the cooked shiitake and ham coarsely.

4. Place all ingredients in a bowl. Add (A) and mix well.

MALABAR NIGHTSHADE

Effective for
Relieving fatigue
Promoting health
Preventing rough skin
Preventing colds

Malabar nightshade is called 'spinach in India.' It contains more vitamins A and C and calcium than barilla, and recently receives a lot of attention as a healthy vegetable. Boil and season with soy sauce or dress with sesame seeds. It is also good as a salad.

Sautéed Malabar Nightshade

Ingredients: 12½ oz (350 g) malabar nightshade / sauce (1 ⅓ Tbsp soy sauce / 2 tsps vinegar / 2 tsps sesame oil / red chili pepper / garlic) / 2 Tbsps dried bonito flakes / 1 Tbsp salad oil

Method: **1.** Wash malabar nightshade and drain.

2. Mince seeded red pepper and garlic to make sauce mixture.

3. Heat oil in a skillet and sauté both sides of malabar nightshade pressing with a spatula.

4. Place in a plate and pour on sauce and top with dried bonito flakes.

Mulukhiya

Effective for
Preventing arteriosclerosis
Preventing hypertension
Preventing osteoporosis
Healthy stomach

Mulukhiya originally comes from Egypt and the name means 'vegetable eaten by a king.' It is highly nutritious. In comparison with spinach, it contains about seven times as much calcium, three times as much vitamin A and eight times as much vitamin B_2. The amount of vitamin C is the same. Mince and add to soup or fry.

Mulukhiya Soup

Ingredients: 7 oz (200 g) mulukhiya / 4⅕ oz (120 g) chicken / 1 clove garlic / 4 Tbsps sake / 2 bouillon cubes / salt and pepper / 1 Tbsp salad oil

Method: **1.** Cut mulukhiya in bite-sized lengths.

2. Cut chicken into small pieces and slice garlic.

3. Heat oil in a pan and sauté garlic and chicken until chicken changes color. Add 3 cups water, sake, crushed bouillon cubes and cook for 15 minutes.

4. Add mulukhiya to (3). Cook for another 7 to 8 minutes, seasoning with salt and pepper.

Sautéed
Malabar Nightshade
Mulukhiya Soup
Chinese-style
Barilla Salad

GREEN TEA

Effective for
Preventing hypertension
Relieving fatigue
Diuretic
Preventing cancer

Green tea contains plenty of vitamin A and vitamin C as well as potassium and minerals. It also has catechin, which is said to lower cholesterol levels and prevent cancer. If you eat green tea instead of brewing it, you can take all of these in an effective way.

Powdered green tea
Green tea (middle grade)

Powdered Green Tea Bavarian

Ingredients for 4 servings: ½ tsp powdered green tea / 2 egg yolks / 2 Tbsps sugar / 1 cup milk / ¼ cup cream / 1 egg white / 1 tsp powdered gelatin / 1 Tbsp white wine

Method: 1. Dissolve powdered gelatin in white wine.

2. In a pan blend egg yolks, sugar and powdered green tea well. Pour milk in slowly a little at a time.

3. Heat the mixture over low heat and cook at temperature below boiling.

4. Remove from heat and add dissolved gelatin. Set the pan in a bowl filled with ice water to chill.

5. When the mixture thickens, fold in whipped cream and the egg white.

6. Pour into a mold moistened with water and chill in the refrigerator.

Powdered Green Tea Milk

Ingredients for 1 serving: ½ tsp powdered green tea / 1 cup milk

Method: Add powdered green tea to milk and blend well with a whisk or spoon.

* If desired, add honey or sugar. Either cold or hot milk is fine.

Smoked Squid and Fish with Green Tea

Ingredients: ½ cup green tea leaves / 1 small squid / 4 pond smelt or sea smelt / salt / lemon / Chinese parsley

Method: 1. Remove tentacles from squid, gut and remove skin. Remove scales from pond smelt and gut.

2. Place squid, tentacles and pond smelt in a bamboo basket. Sprinkle with salt and set aside for 20 minutes.

3. Spread aluminum foil in a pan and place green tea leaves on the bottom. Place a grill on the foil and put squid, tentacles and pond smelt on it. Wrap the foil around the contents and cook for 10 to 15 minutes.

4. Cut squid in rings and arrange with tentacles and pond smelt on a platter. Garnish with Chinese parsley. Sprinkle with lemon juice.

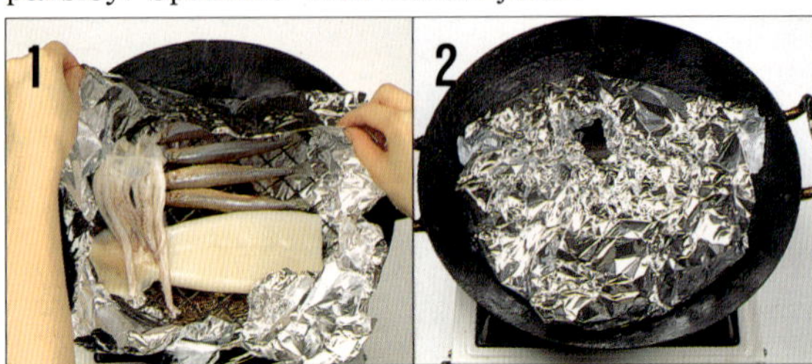

Two Kinds of Green Tea Condiments

Good for sprinking over rice or spaghetti. Also used for the batter of tempura.

Powdered Green Tea and Sesame Seeds (photo, left)

Ingredients and method: Wrap ¼ cup white sesame seeds in a paper towel and heat in a microwave oven for 30 seconds. Grind coarsely. Mix with 2 tsps of powdered green tea and salt.

Powdered Green Tea and Dried Young Sardine (photo, right)

Ingredients and method: Wrap ¼ cup dried young sardine in paper towel. Heat in a microwave oven for 1 minute to dry. Crush with the bottom of a glass. Mix with 2 tsps powdered green tea.

Powdered
Green Tea Milk
Smoked Squid and Fish
with Green Tea
Powdered Green Tea Bavarian

BEANS and NUTS

Beans and nuts are good sources of vegetable albumin as well as vitamins B_1 and B_2. Protein is indispensable for building muscles, and it helps remove surplus fat. Vitamin B_1 relieves fatigue and stimulates brain activity. Vitamin B_2 protects skin and eyes. Let's eat more beans and nuts.

SOYBEANS

For prevention of adult diseases and keeping skin young !

Also called 'meat in the field,' soybeans are equivalent to animal products in terms of protein quality. A hundred grams of soybeans contains 35 grams of protein. They are also rich in fat, most of which is polyunsaturated fat or linoleic acid, and it plays an important role of lowering the cholesterol level in blood. Moreover soybeans have vitamins B_1, B_2, E, and iron, calcium and dietary fiber.

Effective for

Preventing hypertension

Preventing arteriosclerosis

Relieving constipation

For constipation prevention and beautiful skin

Healthy Soybean Salad

Ingredients: ¼ cup dried soybeans / ½ carrot / ¼ cup green peas / 4 small onions / 1 cup cottage cheese / 1⅓ Tbsps lemon juice / salt and pepper / fresh thyme

Method: 1. Soak soybeans in water overnight. Boil until tender.

2. Cut carrot into ⅛ inch (5 mm) dices. Boil carrot and green peas in salted water. Drain and season with salt and pepper.

3. Slice onions into thin rings and soak in water.

4. Put drained soybeans, carrot and green peas in a bowl. Add cottage cheese, lemon juice, salt and pepper and mix lightly.

5. Top with sliced onion and sprinkle with fresh thyme.

Combination of vegetable and animal proteins

Soybeans and Chicken Wings

Ingredients: ½ cup dried soybeans / 4 chicken wings / ½ leek / 1 clove ginger / 4 Tbsps soy sauce / 4 Tbsps sake / 4 Tbsps mirin (sweet sake) / 2 Tbsps salad oil

Method: 1. Soak soybeans in water overnight. Boil until almost tender.

2. Wash chicken wings in boiling water. Mince leek and ginger.

3. Heat oil in a pan and add ginger, leek and chicken wings. Brown wings lightly.

4. Add boiled soybeans and sake. Pour water to cover half the amount of ingredients and cook for 20 minutes. When the liquid is boiled down, add soy sauce and mirin.

* If desired, add 1 minced tomato.

Miso Soup with Ground Soybeans

Ingredients and method: 1. Soak ¼ cup soybeans in water overnight and boil until tender. Put soybeans and 2 cups of dashi soup through a blender to liquefy.

2. Pour boiling water over 1 fried tofu to remove the excess oil. Cut in half and then crosswise into thin strips. Cut daikon 2⅘ oz (80 g) into thin strips.

3. Put fried tofu, daikon and dashi in a pan and cook for 7 minutes. Add (1) and cook for another 5 minutes.

4. Add 3½ Tbsps miso and bring to a boil. Pour in a serving bowl and sprinkle with ½ a sliced scallion and shichimi spices.

ADZUKI BEANS

Historically used to prevent beriberi and regulate intestines

Effective for

Relieving fatigue

Relieving constipation

Diuretic

Adzuki beans contain vitamin B_1, which promotes metabolic activities and relieves fatigue, iron, calcium, potassium, and minerals. It is effective in preventing anemia which is caused by the shortage of iron. It also has saponin and dietary fiber, quickens the action of the bowels and increases discharge of urine.

Healthy porridge effective in nursing a hangover

Rice Porridge with Adzuki Beans

Historically, it was customary for Japanese to eat this porridge on January 15 to pray for a good harvest.

Ingredients: 1 cup adzuki beans / 1 cup rice / salt / mitsuba (trefoil)

Method: **1.** Rinse rice and soak in water over 30 minutes.

2. Wash adzuki beans well and cook in enough water for 20 to 30 minutes.

3. Cover rice with 5 times its volume in water and cook over high flame.

4. When it comes to a boil, add boiled adzuki beans. Simmer over low heat for 50 to 55 minutes. Season with salt.

5. Turn off the heat, and leave it covered for a while. Serve in bowls, topping with mitsuba.

Plenty of dietary fiber

Adzuki Beans Braised with Squash

Ingredients: 1 cup adzuki beans / 7 oz (200 g) squash (Hokkaido or similar variety) / 2½ Tbsps sugar / ¾ tsp salt / 1 Tbsp butter

Method: 1. Wash adzuki beans well and cook in a sufficient amount of water until tender.

2. Remove seeds from squash and cut into bite-sized pieces. Pare skin randomly to cook well.

3. Place boiled adzuki beans, squash, sugar and salt in a saucepan. Add enough water to cover and cook at moderate heat for 17 to 18 minutes.

4. When squash becomes tender, add butter. Toss lightly.

∗Sweet potatoes may be substituted for sqaush. If desired, change the amount of sugar.

Marinated Adzuki Beans

Ingredients: 1 cup adzuki beans / 4 slices bacon / 6 small onions / ½ lemon / 2 Tbsps vinegar / salt and pepper / 1 Tbsp salad oil / chervil

Method: 1. Wash adzuki beans well. Add a sufficient amount of water and cook until tender.

2. Slice onions and separate into rings. Slice lemon. Cut bacon in strips.

3. Heat oil in a skillet and fry bacon until crispy. Turn off the heat and add vinegar.

4. Combine adzuki beans, onions, lemon, salt and pepper in a flat container and add (3) including the liquid..

5. Set aside for 20 minutes. Serve in a plate topped with chervil.

Effects of Adzuki Beans / Plenty of vitamin B_1 and saponin

Adzuki beans contain vitamin A and a large quantity of vitamin B_1. When boiled most of vitamin B_1 is dissolved into the liquid, and it has been used to prevent and treat beriberi historically. Saponin promotes urination, keeps the bowels active, and increases the secretion of milk. When a mother's breasts are dry, it has often been suggested that she should eat cooked adzuki beans together with the liquid it was cooked in. When one feels sick from drinking too much, saponin is also effective in preventing nausea. For a hangover, cook ⅓ oz (10 g) adzuki beans in 1 cup of water; boil down up to half the amount; drink the strained liquid two or three times a day. It works as an antinausea medicine. You may add a little salt to it to make it easier to drink.

Effective for
Preventing arteriosclerosis
Relieving constipation
Preventing cancer

GREEN SOYBEANS

Compared with mature soybeans, green soybeans contain less protein, fat, calcium, and dietary fiber, but they have vitamins A and C, which the former lacks. They are recommended for those who are concerned about colon cancer.

Green Soybeans Mixed with Grated Daikon

Ingredients: 2 cups green soybeans in the pod / 2 cups grated daikon / salt / sweet vinegar (2½ Tbsps vinegar / 1 Tbsp sugar / dash salt) / water pepper

Method: 1. Boil green soybeans in the pod in salted water for 5 to 6 minutes. Drain in a bamboo basket and shell.

2. Mix vinegar, sugar and salt well to make sweet vinegar.

3. Combine green soybeans with grated daikon and pour sweet vinegar over all. Top with water pepper.

Effective for
Relieving constipation
Preventing colds
Relieving fatigue

BROAD BEANS

Broad beans are rich in vitamins B_1, B_2, and dietary fiber. Fresh broad beans are nutritious and tasty, so choose new green ones.

Broad Bean Salad with Yogurt

Ingredients: 3 cups broad beans in the pod / 2 red peppers / salt / yogurt sauce (¾ cup plain yogurt / dash salt / 2 tsps lemon juice / 1 tsp mustard paste)

Method: 1. Shell broad beans and boil in salted water for about 3 minutes. Peel the outer skin.

2. Remove seeds from red peppers and blanch. Cut into ¼ inch (7 mm) dices.

3. Combine plain yogurt, salt, lemon juice, and mustard paste to make yogurt sauce.

4. Place broad beans in a bowl and scatter red peppers on them. Pour yogurt sauce over all.

KIDNEY BEANS

There are a variety of kidney beans. Kidney beans contain protein, fat, calcium, and vitamin B_1, which is effective in preventing beriberi.

Effective for
- Relieving constipation
- Preventing beriberi
- Preventing obesity

Kidney Beans Cooked with Apricots

Ingredients: 3½ oz (100 g) cooked kidney beans (available on the market) / ½ cup frozen green peas / 4 dried apricots / brandy or black tea / 1 Tbsp sugar / mint

Method: **1.** Thaw green peas by pouring boiling water over them.

2. Soak dried apricots in brandy or black tea, and then cut into quarters.

3. Put kidney beans, green peas and apricots in a pot. Add sugar and water to just a little below the surface of the ingredients. Cook over low heat.

4. Serve in a bowl and top with mint.

* Adjust the taste with the amount of sugar. If you use fresh green peas, remove peas from pods and parboil in salted water.

GREEN PEAS

Green peas have dietary fiber and vitamin B_1. They are one of the most popular legumes and can be cooked in a variety of ways; boiled with sugar, strained for potage, etc.

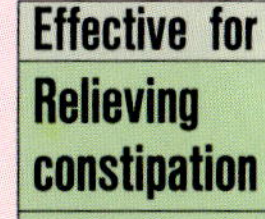
Effective for
- Relieving constipation
- Relieving fatigue
- Preventing arteriosclerosis

Green Peas Cooked with Onions

Ingredients: 2 cups green peas in the pod / 4 slices bacon / 8 small onions / 1 Tbsp butter / 1 bouillon cube / 1 bay leaf / salt and pepper

Method: **1.** Blanch bacon and cut into ⅜ inch (1 cm) lengths.

2. Put green peas, bacon, peeled whole onions in a pot. Add water to cover half of the ingredients, a crushed bouillon cube, butter, a bay leaf and cook over a high flame.

3. When it comes to a boil, lower heat and cover with a lid. Cook slowly until the liquid evaporates, taking care not to brown.

4. Season with salt and pepper.

GINKGO NUTS

Full of vitality with the germination rate of 100%

Effective for

Providing energy

Stifling coughs

Controling enuresis

Although the main component is starch, ginkgo nuts contain protein, vitamins A, B_1 and C. Traditionally they have been known as a tonic and used in Chinese medicine for asthma, bronchitis, frequent urination, and enuresis. Overeating them causes dizziness and is poisonous, so eat a moderate amount.

Perk yourself up with ginkgo nuts

Fried Ginkgo Nuts

Ingredients: ½ cup ginkgo nuts / 4 slices whitefish (sea bream, cutlassfish or Spanish mackerel) / 2 tsps sake / flour / 1 egg white / salt / oil for deep-frying

Method: **1.** Cut whitefish into bite-sized slices. Sprinkle with salt and sake and set aside for 20 minutes.

2. Shell ginkgo nuts and boil in salted water. Remove outer skins of the ginkgo nuts by rubbing with a ladle and remove into cold water. Pat off water and cut into slices.

3. Coat fish slices with flour, egg white, and ginkgo slices in this order. Deep-fry in oil (350°F/175°C) until golden brown.

*Before deep-frying, press fish and ginkgo nuts lightly with hands to hold their shape. Canned boiled ginkgo nuts can be substituted.

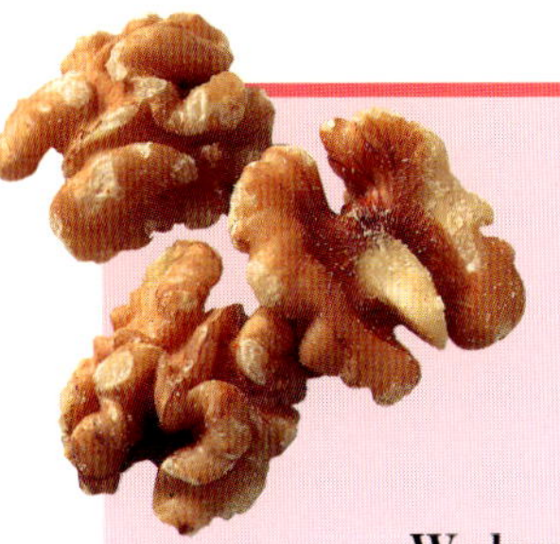

WALNUTS

Walnuts are a good source of vegetable protein, fat and vitamins B_1 and E. They are said to make skin beautiful and hair black. In China they are popular as food for beauty. They are also effective in keeping healthy brains.

Effective for
- Providing energy
- Relieving constipation
- Beautiful skin

Walnut Salad

Ingredients: ½ cup shelled walnuts / 1 small head lettuce / salt / dressing (2 Tbsps vinegar / 2 Tbsps walnut oil / salt and pepper) / thyme

Method: 1. Blanch walnuts and chop coarsely.

2. Tear lettuce into bite-sized pieces and put into salted water until soft. Wash the pieces in water and drain.

3. Dissolve salt and pepper in vinegar. Add walnut oil little by little to make dressing.

4. Toss lettuce with the dressing. Top with walnuts and thyme.

* Olive oil or salad oil can be substituted for walnut oil.

PEANUTS

They have almost the same nutritious content as walnuts. They are popular as a snack and used in cakes and salads. They are oxidizable, so keep in an airtight container.

Effective for
- Relieving constipation
- Promoting appetite
- Providing energy

Peanut Pudding

Ingredients for 4 servings: ¾ cup peanuts / 2 cups soft breadcrumbs / 3 Tbsps butter / ½ cup sugar / 2 egg whites / 2 egg yolks / ⅓ cup milk / vanilla extract / drained cherries

Method: 1. Set aside some peanuts for garnish. Chop the rest finely. Keep butter at room temperature.

2. Cream butter in a bowl until smooth. Add sugar and egg yolks and beat well.

3. Add to (2) in this order: vanilla extract, soft breadcrumbs, chopped peanuts and milk and blend well. Then beat egg whites until stiff and fold in.

4. (Using extra butter and flour) Butter a mold and sprinkle with flour. Pour (3) in the mold. Steam for about 16 minutes . Insert a bamboo skewer in the middle and if it comes out clean, it is done.

5. Place on a serving platter and decorate with peanuts and drained cherries.

SESAME SEEDS

Ideal nutritious food popular all over the world

White sesame seeds

Effective for

Providing energy

Preventing arteriosclerosis

Preventing anemia

Black sesame seeds

Sesame seeds have plenty of good quality protein and fat, in fact the highest content of all vegetable foods. Moreover they are rich in vitamins B_1, E, iron and calcium. In Turkey, it is said that the armed forces employed sesame seeds as provisions for their nutritious value. In China, sesame seeds have been valued as a miracle drug for longevity, energy and constipation. We should make use of sesame seeds in our daily diet.

Source of healthy life

Arabic-style Sesame Seed Salad

Popular cooking in the Arab States, where sesame seeds are used alone. As they have peculiar taste, let's make them into a sauce.

Ingredients: sauce (1 cup white sesame seeds / 2 tsps lemon juice / ⅓ tsp salt / dash pepper / ⅓ cup salad oil / parsley) / fresh vegetable leaves (watercress or wild chicory)

Method: **1.** Toast white sesame seeds and grind coarsely in an earthenware mortar.

2. In a bowl, add lemon juice, salt, pepper and salad oil and mix well as in the photo. Sprinkle with chopped parsley.

3. Toss fresh vegetables with the sauce and serve.

Arabic-style Sesame Seed Salad

Sesame Seed Soup

Sesame Seed Candy

Healthy snack

Sesame Seed Candy

A Korean-style sweet candy. In Korea, sesame seeds, walnuts, and pine nuts are often used in cakes for their medicinal effects.

Ingredients: 1 cup white sesame seeds / 6 dried apricots / 1 tsp brandy / 1 cup brown sugar / salad oil

Method: **1.** Sprinkle dried apricots with brandy and set aside for 20 minutes. Chop finely.

2. Put brown sugar and a little water in a saucepan. Dissolve sugar over low heat and simmer for 2 to 3 minutes.

3. Remove from heat and add toasted sesame seeds and apricots and mix well. (photo 1)

4. Remove (3) to an oiled flat container and set leave until set. (photo 2)

5. Cut into bite-sized pieces and remove to a serving dish.

With wakame, full of fiber

Sesame Seed Soup

Ingredients: 2 tsps white sesame seeds / ⅓ oz (10 g) dried wakame seaweed / 1 leek / 1 clove ginger / 2 bouillon cubes / 2 Tbsps sake / dash salt and soy sauce / 1 Tbsp sesame oil

Method: **1.** Toast white sesame seeds and grind in an earthenware mortar.

2. Soak dried wakame in water. Cut into bite-sized pieces.

3. Cut leek into chunks. Pare ginger and chop finely.

4. Heat sesame oil in a pan and fry leek and ginger until flavored. Add crushed bouillion cubes, sake, 3 cups water and simmer.

5. When it comes to a boil, add wakame and ground sesame seeds. Season with salt and soy sauce.

* For a variation, you may fry ⅔ oz (20 g) to 1 oz (30 g) chicken or beef (per person) together with leek and ginger.

MUSHROOMS

Mushrooms have not been thought of as a particularly good source of nutrients. But actually mushrooms rank rather high in nutritive value. They have a good deal of dietary fiber and have recently attracted the world's attention as a health food. Regardless of volume, there is no fear of putting on weight. They activate the bowels, get rid of excess fat and cholesterol, and prevent colon cancer. The effects assure us of a healthy life.

CLOUD EAR MUSHROOM
(Kikurage mushroom)

Plenty of dietary fiber, good for bowel movement

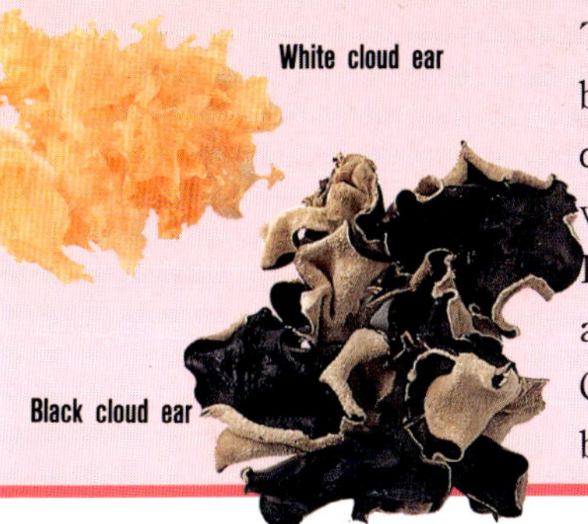

There are two varieties of cloud ears, black and white. Both have a good deal of dietary fiber and no calories. They contain vitamin B_1, B_2, calcium, and potassium. Black cloud ears are especially rich in iron and effective for preventing anemia. In Chinese medicine, they are used to purify blood and cure hemorrhoids and ulcers.

Effective for
Losing weight
Making skin beautiful
Preventing arteriosclerosis

Known in China as a medicine for perpetual youth and longevity

Sweet Cloud Ear Soup

Ingredients: 1 cloud ear (⅔~1 oz) (20~25 g) / ¾ cup rock sugar / edible flowers

Method: **1.** Soak cloud ear in water. Remove stems and break in small pieces.

2. Put rock sugar and 3 cups water in a saucepan and cook until sugar is dissolved.

3. Add cloud ear and bring to a boil. Place the pan in water until cold and then chill in refrigerator.

4. Serve in a bowl and garnish with edible flowers.

Ten times iron of spinach / Crispy taste

Chinese-style Black Cloud Ear Salad

Ingredients: ⅓ oz (10 g) black cloud ear or 8 fresh ones / 2 small green pepper / 2 small red pepper / 1½ Tbsps peanuts / 1½ inch (4 cm) white stalk of leek / salt / juice of ginger / 1⅓ Tbsps sesame oil / 2 Tbsps soy sauce

Method: **1.** Soak dried black cloud ears in water. Remove stems and cut into strips.

2. Remove stems and seeds from peppers and cut into julienne strips.

3. Blanch (1) and (2) in salted water. Put them in water and drain.

4. Arrange drained cloud ears and green peppers in a plate and sprinkle with chopped peanuts. Top with blanched leek.

5. Combine ginger juice, sesame oil with soy sauce and pour over all.

SHIITAKE MUSHROOM

For losing weight and preventing adult diseases

Effective for

Preventing arteriosclerosis

Preventing hypertension

Preventing cancer

Shiitake mushrooms contain eritadenine, which lowers cholesterol levels and lentinan, which prevents the increase of cancer cells. Dried shiitake mushrooms, especially those dried in the sun, are a good source of vitamin D, which helps the absorption of calcium. Incidentally, any sun dried foods have vitamin D.

Dried Shiitake

Taste and flavor are outstanding / Indispensable for supple blood vessels

Spanish-style Shiitake Mushroom Casserole

Ingredients: 12 fresh shiitake mushrooms / ½ onion / 1 clove garlic / 2 tomatoes / 4 Tbsps soft breadcrumbs / 2 tsps chopped parsley / salt and pepper / 2 tsps butter / 1½ Tbsps salad oil

Method: 1. Separate stems from shiitake and cut into slices.

2. Chop onion and garlic finely. Blanch and peel tomatoes. Discard stalk ends and seeds and then cut coarsly.

3. Heat oil in a pan and fry onion and garlic. Add shiitake stems and tomatoes and continue to fry. Season with salt and pepper.

4. Place shiitake tops, (3) and breadcrumbs mixed with parsley in a buttered heatproof casserole. Top with butter and bake in an oven (400°F/200°C) for 7 to 8 minutes.

Tempura from non-caloric mushrooms

Battered and Deep-fried Shiitake Mushroom

Ingredients: 12 fresh shiitake mushrooms / batter (1 egg / dash salt / 1½ Tbsps water / ½ cup flour / 1 Chinese parsley) / salt or soy sauce / oil for deep-frying

Method: 1. Cut off the stems of shiitake. Chop Chinese parsley finely.

2. Beat egg with salt and water. Add sifted flour and Chinese parsley.

3. Dip shiitake in the batter. Deep-fry in frying oil (350°F/175°C) for about 2 minutes.

4. Place on a plate and serve with salt or soy sauce.

* You can also serve with vinegared soy sauce or tomato sauce. Parsley may also be substituted for Chinese parsley.

Dried shiitake mushrooms are also delicious

Shiitake Mushroom Dumplings

Ingredients: 12 fresh shiitake mushrooms / 12 prawns / 4 sea scallops / dash salt / grated ginger / 1 tsp sesame oil / 1 egg white / 1½ tsps cornstarch / chopped parsley / lettuce leaves / ponzu sauce mixed with soy sauce

Method: 1. Remove stems from shiitake.

2. Shell prawns, devein and cut up. Cut scallops finely.

3. Mix the following ingredients well: (2), salt, ginger, sesame oil, egg white and ½ tsp cornstarch. Divide into 12.

4. Turn shiitake tops upside down and sprinkle with the rest of cornstarch and top with (3). Place shiitake balls on lettuce leaves on a plate. Steam for 7 to 8 minutes. Sprinkle with parsley and serve hot with ponzu.

Flavorful diet food

Shimeji (Oyster Mushrooms) Mixed with Shiso (Perilla)

Ingredients and method: 1. Cut stems off 2 packs of shimeji. Tear thick stalks into strips. Cut a 5¼ oz (150 g) chicken breast into thin strips. Sprinkle shimeji and chicken each with 1 Tbsp of sake and sauté separately. Set aside.

2. Wash 8 shiso leaves in water. Pat off water and cut into julienne strips.

3. Combine 1⅓ Tbsps of vinegar and soy sauce and toss with chicken and shimeji. Top with shiso leaves.

* For variation, white fish or squid can also be substituted for chicken.

HERBS and SPICES

Herbs and spices improve the flavor of savory dishes. They stimulate the appetite and promote the secretion of digestive juices. Hot spices like chilis stimulate nerves, encourage metabolism, and prevent obesity. Let's try to make good use of more herbs and spices in the daily menu.

PARSLEY

Too nutritious to be used only for garnish

Among vegetables the vitamin A content of parsley is second to shiso (perilla) leaves. Parsley has plenty of vitamin C, iron, and calcium. Even a small quantity can supply sufficient nutrition. Its distinctive fragrance contains an element which stimulates the appetite and relieves fatigue.

Effective for
- **Preventing anemia**
- **Relieving fatigue**
- **Increasing appetite**

If sautéed in oil, vitamin A will easily be absorbed

Sautéed Parsley

Ingredients: 4 parsley sprays / a bit of carrot / salt and pepper / 2 tsps salad oil

Method: 1. Wash parsley well. Tear leaves and pat off water with a paper towel.

2. Cut carrot into 2 inch (5 cm) length strips.

3. Heat oil in a skillet and sauté parsley and carrot quickly and season with salt and pepper.

* Thick stems of parsley may be cut up and cooked together. Vitamin A contained in parsley is assimilated easily if it is taken with oil. Parsley is good for not only sautéeing but also deep-frying. When deep-frying, keep the oil temperature around 320°F/160°C.

WATERCRESS

Plenty of calcium, which calms nerves

With a pleasant, slightly hot taste, watercress is a useful source of vitamins A and C, and calcium. When exhausted, it is effective for recovering from fatigue. Like parsley, it is an excellent accompaniment to salad and steak.

Effective for
- **Preventing colds**
- **Aiding digestion**
- **Increasing appetite**

Don't discard the stems / Eat it whole

Watercress Salad

Ingredients: a bunch of watercress / 3 cabbage leaves / salt / French dressing (2 Tbsps vinegar / 2 Tbsps salad oil / dash salt and pepper)

Method: 1. Shred cabbage and sprinkle with salt and rub. Wash in water and drain.

2. Tear watercress leaves, wash and drain. Cut thick stems into 1 inch (2.5 cm) lengths. Blanch in salted water.

3. Make French dressing by combining vinegar, salt, pepper and oil in this order and blend well.

4. In a bowl, toss cabbage, watercress leaves and stems with dressing.

* An easy method of making dressing: In a small bottle, put the ingredients of dressing and shake well before using.

Effective for
- Toning the body
- Aiding digestion
- Increasing appetite

MINT

An aromatic plant used to flavor a number of dishes. It is said that mint promotes digestion and tones the system. It also can be used for herb tea. Oil of peppermint is distilled from the stems and leaves.

Mint Tea

Ingredients for 1 serving: 5~6 mint leaves / ½ cup boiling water

Method: 1. Put mint leaves in a warmed teapot, pour boiling water in and cover. Set aside for 2 to 3 minutes.

2. Pour through a strainer into a warmed cup.

*If desired, add honey or sugar. When using dried mint, add 1 tsp mint per 1 cup.

Effective for
- Toning the body
- Sterilizing
- Relieving stress

BASIL

The leaves are used with spaghetti, tomato, soups and salads. Chinese medicine uses the decocted juice to wash the eyes.

Basil Sandwiches

Ingredients: 4 basil leaves / 4 slices bread for sandwiches / 2 slices cheese / 2 tsps butter

Method: 1. Butter bread and cover with cheese slices and basil. Top with remaining bread.

2. Wrap with plastic food wrap or paper towel for 10 minutes. Cut into pieces.

*Hard-boiled egg, raw ham, smoked salmon may also be used.

Aloe is effective for a healthy stomach

Traditionally, aloe has been a popular remedy for burns. It has also been said to put the stomach in order. It can be made into juice or eaten raw as sashimi. The skin is bitter, so it may be peeled before using.

Aloe Juice (1 serving)

Ingredients and method: Pare the skin of ¼ an aloe leaf and take out the gelatinous parts. In a juicer, put the gelatinous parts, a few komatsuna leaves, 1½ inch (4 cm) stalk of celery, ½ spray of parsley, ¼ a small tomato, 2 wedged pieces of apple and blend all. Put a few drops of lemon juice and ¼ tsp honey and garnish with a fresh aloe leaf.

AOJISO
(Green perilla)

Aojiso has the highest vitamin A content among vegetables. It also has plenty of vitamin C, which is effective for preventing colds, iron and dietary fiber. The aromatic leaves work as a food preservative.

Effective for
- Preventing colds
- Stifling coughs
- Healthy stomach

Miso Wrapped in Aojiso

Ingredients: 20 aojiso (perilla) leaves / miso paste 《2 Tbsps miso (fermented bean paste) / ½ Tbsp mirin (sweet sake) / ½ Tbsp sugar / 2 Tbsps dashi soup (see inside front cover)》/ 1 tsp salad oil

Method: **1.** Wash perilla leaves in water and drain thoroughly.

2. In a saucepan, combine miso, sugar and dashi soup. Cook over a low flame and mix well until it thickens.

3. Place (2) on each perilla leaf and roll tightly with care not to allow air in.

4. Skewer two together with chopsticks and sauté both sides for a short time.

KINOME
(Pepper leaf buds)

Kinome is a new bud leaf of the Japanese pepper. The aromatic leaves are used for dressing vegetables and removing fish odors. They contain vitamins A and C.

Effective for
- Increasing appetite
- Preventing colds
- Healthy stomach

Salad with Kinome

Ingredients: ¼ cup kinome / 9 oz (250 g) raw white fish slices / 4 cabbage leaves / ½ carrot / 4 fresh shiitake mushrooms / salt / dressing (1 Tbsp lemon juice / dash salt / 1 Tbsp soy sauce / 1 tsp sake)

Method: **1.** Shred cabbage and carrot into 2 inch (5 cm) lengths. Sprinkle with salt and squeeze. Wash and drain.

2. Discard stems from shiitake and grill lightly. Cut in julienne strips.

3. Toss (1) and (2) with dressing, top with white fish slices and scatter leaf buds over all lavishly.

Fresh Aloe Slices

Ingredients and method: **1.** Wash a small aloe leaf well and cut into thin slices.

2. Peel 1½ inch (4 cm) daikon thinly all the way around. Roll it and cut into strips. Chill in cold water and drain.

3. Place daikon on a plate and top with aloe slices as shown in the photo. Put an aloe in the center for garnish and serve with soy sauce and Japanese horseradish.

GINGER

Immediate relief when coming down with a cold / Suppress a cough and warm up

Effective for

Increasing appetite

Aiding digestion

Improving circulation

Ginger has a characteristic hot flavor and pungent taste. It contains potassium and is used in various forms in cookery and medicine. It is the oldest spice in Japan. In Chinese medicine, it is used to prevent nausea, stimulate the appetite, improve blood circulation, cure headaches, and stifle a cough.

The essence of ginger increases the appetite

Ginger Jam

Ingredients: 7 oz (200 g) ginger / ½ lemon peel (white part) / 3½~5¼ oz (100~150 g) sugar (50~75% the weight of ginger)

Method: 1. Pare ginger and chop finely. Cover with water and bring to a boil. Pour in extra water and bring to a boil again. Repeat 2 or 3 times. Drain.

2. Chop the white peel of lemon finely.

3. Put ginger, sugar, lemon peel and 1 Tbsp water in a saucepan and cook over low heat for about 20 to 30 minutes until very thick.

*In refrigerator, it can be stored for 3 months.

Healthy snack for the prevention of colds

Ginger Coated with Granulated Sugar

Ingredients: 5¼ oz (150 g) ginger / 2⅔ oz (75 g) sugar (50% the weight of ginger) / granulated sugar for coating

Method: 1. Cut ginger with skin into slices. Cover with water and bring to a boil. Pour in extra water and bring to a boil again. Repeat 2 or 3 times. Drain.

2. Put ginger in a saucepan and coat ginger with sugar.

3. Add a little water and boil down over low heat with care not to burn.

4. Spread ginger one by one in a flat container and set aside for 1 or 2 days. Sprinkle with granulated sugar while ginger is still wet.

GARLIC

Cures all sorts of ills, indispensable for developing stamina

It has been prohibited to bring garlic and leeks in the temple, because they are too strong and powerful, and disturb the training of priests. Garlic contains a substance that interferes with the formation of blood clots and in addition may help reduce blood cholesterol. Be careful not to overeat. Try to eat a moderate quantity.

Effective for

- **Relieving fatigue**
- **Preventing colds**
- **Improving circulation**

A garlic clove a day keeps the doctor away

Garlic Pickled in Soy Sauce

Ingredients: 3～4 pieces of garlic / sauce 《2 cups soy sauce / ¼ cup mirin (sweet sake) / 1 tsp juice of ginger》

Method: 1. Separate garlic into individual cloves and peel off the outer layers of skin.

2. Put garlic in a jar sterilized in boiling water and pour sauce over contents (photo).

3. Cover with a lid and set aside for more than 3 weeks in a cold and dark place.

＊ Can be stored for a long period. If spicy, chop garlic finely before serving. The mirin in sauce can be substituted for sake. If desired, some red chili pepper may be added.

Recommended when depressed

Whole Garlic Steamed

Ingredients: 1 whole garlic / 1 shiso (perilla) leaf

Method: 1. Wrap the whole garlic with plastic wrap.

2. Place in a microwave oven and cook for 1 minute. Spread shiso leaf in a plate and put garlic on it.

＊ When cooked in a microwave oven, the texture of garlic becomes soft like potatoes and the strong flavor mellows.

WASABI
(Japanese horseradish)

The strong bite increases the appetite and helps digestion.

Effective for
Aiding digestion
Increasing appetite
Diuresis

Generally, the pungent root is used, but the leaves and flowers are also used for cookery from spring to summer. It is a good source of vitamin C and dietary fiber. Historically, it has been said that the pungent taste helps digestion, counteracts poison, and increases the discharge of urine.

For stimulating the appetite

Pickled Wasabi Flowers

Ingredients: 2 bunches of wasabi flowers / sauce (½ cup soy sauce / ¼ ~ ⅓ cup sake)

Method: 1. Place wasabi flowers in a bamboo basket, pour hot water over them and drain. Cover the basket with a bowl and set aside until cooled to improve the hot taste.

2. Discard stems and cut the remaining parts into 1 inch (2.5 cm) lengths. Pour sauce over them and set aside for a day.

*Eat as they are, use in salads or stir-fry for variation.

For relieving fatigue

Vinegared Wasabi Root

Ingredients: 1 small wasabi root / 4 inches (10 cm) kombu kelp / ½ daikon / ½ small carrot / salt / vinegar sauce (½ cup vinegar / 4 Tbsps sugar / dash salt)

Method: 1. Scrub the root and scrape away the outer skin. Cut into 2 inch (5 cm) length strips.

2. Cut kombu into ⅜ inch (1 cm) wide pieces.

3. Quarter daikon and cut into ⅜ inch (1 cm) thick slices. Cut carrot into thin slices and shape like flowers using a cutter. Soak all in salted water until soft. Squeeze out water.

4. Mix wasabi, kombu and vegetables in vinegar sauce and set aside for 1 week.

*May keep in the refrigerator for 2~3 months.

MYOGA
(Japanese ginger)

The color, flavor and taste of myoga will make you feel refreshed in summer. It stimulates the appetite and in Chinese medicine it is used to allay fevers and control irregular menstruation.

Effective for
- Increasing appetite
- Aiding digestion
- Regular menstruation

Myoga Ginger Pickled in Sweet Vinegar

Ingredients: 20 pieces of myoga / a bit of vinegar / dash salt / sweet vinegar (½ cup vinegar / ½ tsp salt / ¼ cup sugar)

Method: **1.** Wash myoga in water and blanch in water flavored with a little vinegar and salt. Drain.

2. Blend salt and sugar with vinegar to make sweet vinegar.

3. Put myoga in the sweet vinegar and set aside for more than 20 minutes until color changes.

* If sugar is not dissolved completely in vinegar, bring it to a boil.

RED CHILI PEPPER

A substance called capsaicin contained in peppers has the effect of warming the body and increasing the appetite. They are a good source of vitamins A and C.

Effective for
- Increasing appetite
- Improving circulation
- Preventing colds

White Fish Stir-fried with Red Chili Pepper

Ingredients: 4 slices white fish (flatfish, cod or sea bass) / 2 red chili peppers / 1 clove garlic / 2 scallions / 3 Tbsps salad oil / salt

Method: **1.** Sprinkle fish slices with salt and set aside for 20 to 30 minutes. Cut into bite-sized pieces.

2. Remove seeds from peppers. Cut garlic into slices. Slice scallions in rings.

3. Heat oil in a pan and fry peppers and garlic until brown. Add fish slices.

4. When fish is cooked season with salt. Sprinkle with chopped scallions.

Seasoned Red Pepper Leaves

Ingredients and method: Tear a bunch of pepper leaves and wash in water and drain. Put in a pan and add ¼ cup soy sauce and 2 Tbsps sake. Boil down over low heat. If desired, add several shredded peppers.

LIGHT-COLORED VEGETABLES

As a source of vitamins, light-colored vegetables are not made much of, but they are a good source of dietary fiber. Enjoying the plain taste of vegetables, we can take as much fiber as we want. Each vegetable has its own effect. For example, cabbage and celery contain plenty of potassium, which promotes the discharge of sodium and prevents high blood pressure. Let's eat a good deal of vegetables to keep stay healthy.

Cabbage Sautéed with Sweet Vinegar

Cabbage Rolled in Aburaage

CABBAGE

Plenty of vitamins C and U,
good for protecting stomach and easing stress

Among the light-colored vegetables, cabbage ranks first in the content of vitamin C. Since we can eat a large quantity at a time, we can take vitamin C effectively. It also has vitamin U, which is said to cure gastric ulcers. However, both vitamins are vulnerable to heat. As they are insoluble in oil, they remain in the liquid when fried or boiled, so don't forget to make use of it.

Effective for
Preventing colds
Relieving fatigue
Preventing stomach ulcers

After drinking alcohol

Cabbage Sautéed with Sweet Vinegar

Ingredients: 4 large cabbage leaves / 1 red chili pepper / 1 clove garlic / sweet vinegar (2 Tbsps vinegar / 2 tsps sugar / 1 tsp soy sauce / dash salt) / 3 Tbsps salad oil

Method: 1. Cut cabbage leaves into 1½ inch (4 cm) square pieces.

2. Remove seeds from red chili pepper. Cut garlic into slices.

3. Heat oil in a skillet and sauté red chili pepper and garlic until flavor comes out.

4. Add cabbage and stir-fry for a short time and combine sweet vinegar. Toss once or twice to season well before serving.

Nutritiously balanced

Cabbage Cooked in Wine Broth

Ingredients: 4 large cabbage leaves / 1 small carrot / 8 small onions / 8 frankfurters / broth (¼ bouillon cube / ½ cup white wine / ½ cup water / 1 bay leaf) / salt and pepper / 1 Tbsp butter

Method: 1. Cut carrot into 2 inch (5 cm) length sticks. Peel onions. Parboil onions and cabbage for 5~6 minutes.

2. Fold cabbage as shown below, and put in a pan together with carrot, onions and frankfurters. Add water, white wine, crushed bouillon cube, bay leaf and simmer.

3. When vegetables are done, season with salt, pepper and butter.

Plenty of calcium

Cabbage Rolled in Aburaage

Ingredients: 4 large cabbage leaves / 2 sheets aburaage (deep-fried tofu) / 16 inches (40 cm) kanpyo (dried gourd strips) / broth《½ cup dashi stock, (see inside front cover) / 1⅓ Tbsps sake / 1⅓ Tbsps mirin (sweet sake)/ 1⅓ Tbsps soy sauce》 / salt

Method: 1. Put cabbage leaves in boiling water until tender, cut out stem portion of leaves and discard.

2. Rinse aburaage in boiling water to get rid of excess oil. Slit around 3 sides opening the aburaage out into a single sheet. Rub kanpyo with salt until soft and boil in water.

3. On a cutting board, place aburaage inside up and spread cabbage leaves on it. Roll together as shown in the photo, and tie with kanpyo in two places.

4. Cook in broth slowly. Cut into two.

ONION

Strong flavor and indispensable for strenghthening the body

Effective for

Increasing stamina

Aiding digestion

Relieving fatigue

Like garlic and leeks, onions have a characteristic pungent odor compound , allyl sulfide, which helps absorption of vitamin B_1 and digestion. The act of chopping or slicing brings its sulfur-containing amino acids into contact with enzymes to form volatile compounds, one of which irritates the eye. To avoid the irritation, you may chill the onions or wet the knife.

Source of stamina

Onions with Raisins

Ingredients: 16 small onions / ¼ cup raisins / 1⅓ Tbsps butter / 1 tsp sugar / salt and pepper

Method: 1. Put peeled onions and other ingredients in a pan and cover with water.

2. Place paper cover over the ingredients and heat at high flame. When it comes to a boil, lower heat and cook slowly.

3. When the liquid is almost gone, remove the paper cover and let it boil down again quickly over a high flame.

*Chopped parsley may be added.

Colorful Italian-style

Marinated Onion

Ingredients: 2 onions / 1 tomato / 1 green pepper / salt / a bit of vinegar / marinade (2 Tbsps vinegar / 4 Tbsps salad oil / dash salt and pepper)

Method: 1. Cut onions into ¼ inch (¾ cm) thick slices and boil in salted and vinegared water for a short time. Drain.

2. Blanch tomato, peel and remove seeds. Remove seeds from green pepper. Cut tomato and green pepper into ⅛ inch (½ cm) square pieces.

3. Combine the ingredients for marinade and blend well.

4. Put onions, tomato and green pepper in the marinade and let stand for 30 minutes.

*If desired, add lemon juice, soy sauce and spices to the marinade.

CHINESE CABBAGE

Together with tofu and daikon, Chinese cabbage is regarded as one of the three treasures of healthy foods. They are said to strengthen lungs. They are a good source of vitamin C and rich in potassium, which discharges salt and prevents high blood pressure.

Effective for
Relieving stress
Preventing hypertension
Preventing constipatio

Korean-style Chinese Cabbage

A special dish with Chinese cabbage, which moves the bowels and prevents colds; leeks and ginger, which make the throat healthy; plus an apple, which contains plenty of dietary fiber and prevents constipation.

Ingredients: 14 oz (400 g) Chinese cabbage (½ big head) / dash salt / mixture 《3 inches (8 cm) leeks / ½ clove garlic / ½ clove ginger / ½ red chili pepper / 1 apple / 2 tsps sesame oil / ½ lemon juice / 1 tsp soy sauce》

Method: 1. Cut the stalk of the Chinese cabbage into bite-sized slices and the leaves roughly. Rub with salt until tender.

2. Chop leek, garlic and ginger finely. Remove seeds from red chili pepper and chop finely. Peel apple, core and grate.

3. Add sesame oil, lemon juice and soy sauce to (2) and mix well. Squeeze water out of Chinese cabbage and toss with the mixture.

NAGANEGI

(Long Onion, a relative of leeks and scallions)

Like onions, the odor compound, allyl sulfide, helps digestion and the absorption of vitamin B_1. They warm the body and the decoction of the chopped naganegi is effective when coming down with a cold.

Effective for
Preventing colds
Aiding digestion
Increasing appetite

Chinese Noodles with Long Onions

Ingredients: 1 lb (450 g) Chinese noodles (4 packs) / 2 scallions / 7 oz (200 g) roasted pork / salt / sauce (½ cup water / 1 tsp Chinese bouillon / 4 Tbsps soy sauce / 1 Tbsp vinegar / 1 Tbsp sesame oil / pinch sugar) / Chinese parsley

Method: 1. Put the ingredients of sauce except vinegar in a pan and bring to a boil. Add vinegar and chill in the refrigerator.

2. Shred scallions into 2 inch (5 cm) lengths. Cut roasted pork into the same size strips.

3. Boil Chinese noodles. When it comes to a boil pour in extra water and boil again. Rinse under a stream of running water and drain in a bamboo basket.

4. Place noodles on a plate and top with roasted pork and scallions. Garnish with Chinese parsley.

5. Pour chilled sauce over noodles and serve.

SPROUTS

Plenty of dietary fiber and low calories

Effective for

Aiding digestion

Preventing constipation

Slowing the aging process

The most familiar sprouts are those of mung bean seeds and soybean seeds. The growth from seed to sprout is accompanied by changes in nutritional value. Sprouts have vitamin C; vitamin E, which slows the aging process of skin; dietary fiber; and a digestive enzyme, amylase. Since they contain a good deal of water and are low in calories, they are strongly recommended to overweight people.

Mung bean sprouts

Soybean sprouts

Korean-style dish, which stimulates appetite

Namuru

Ingredients: 1 pack soybean sprouts / dash salt / mixture《1 clove ginger / ½ clove garlic / 4 inches (10 cm) scallion / 1 tsp vinegar / 2 tsps soy sauce / 1 tsp ground white sesame seeds / dash powdered red chili pepper and pepper》

Method: 1. Remove root hairs from soybean sprouts. Blanch in salted water. Spread in a bamboo basket and let cool.

2. Mince ginger, garlic and scallion and combine with other ingredients of mixture.

3. Drain soy bean sprouts well and toss with the mixture.

*Boil sprouts for a few minutes until a little softer than al dente. They will not lose vitamin C.

Relief from constipation

Curried Sprout Salad

Ingredients: 2 packs mung bean sprouts / 4 slices ham / dash salt / dressing《4 Tbsps French dressing (p.37) / a little minced garlic / 1 tsp curry powder》 / mint or any herb

Method: 1. Remove germs and root hairs from mung bean sprouts. Blanch in salted water. Spread in a bamboo basket and let cool.

2. Cut ham into strips.

3. Put drained mung bean sprouts in a bowl. Top with ham and garnish with mint.

4. Pour dressing over all before serving.

ALFALFA

Reduce blood cholesterol

Alfalfa sprouts are very popular as a diet food. Like mung bean sprouts, they are rich in vitamin C, dietary fiber, and have a digestive enzyme, amylase. They have attracted public attention recently, since it has been found that they reduce blood cholesterol.

Effective for
Preventing obesity
Aiding digestion
Curing of wounds

Vitamin C salad

Alfalfa with Vinegared Miso

Ingredients: 4 cups alfalfa sprouts / mixture 《2½ Tbsps miso (fermented bean paste) / 2 tsps sugar / 1 Tbsp mirin (sweet sake) / 4 Tbsps dashi soup (see inside front cover) / 1 Tbsp vinegar / a little pasted mustard》 / chopped scallions for garnish

Method: 1. Wash alfalfa sprouts under running water and drain.

2. Put miso, sugar, mirin and dashi soup in a saucepan. Heat over a low flame and mix well until smooth and glossy. Let it cool and then mix in vinegar and pasted mustard.

3. Combine alfalfa sprouts with mixture and sprinkle with chopped scallions.

*Wash alfalfa quickly so as not to lose vitamin C.

A Story of Sprouts

Seeds need only water and air to grow. In that way, they are a clean vegetable and a perfect natural food. In Japan, they have been valued to complement the shortage of vegetables. They were indispensable provisions of warriors when they confined themselves to the castle. The most familiar sprouts are those of soybean seeds, mung bean seeds and alfalfa, but buckwheat, wheat and daikon also have seeds that will germinate to yeild edible shoots. The length of soybean sprouts is about 4 inches (10 cm) and others are about 2 inches (5 cm). In the case of daikon sprouts, choose crispy ones with the length of about 4 inches (10 cm). Vitamin C in the sprouts increases when they are spread in a bamboo basket and exposed to the sun (photo). But take care not to leave them long as they tend to wilt. Soybean sprouts are quite different from others in that they have plenty of protein, fat and vitamin E. It is because beans are attached to the sprouts. Generally, sprouts remain crispy when heated, and give a volume to the dish. Since they are low in calories, they are the best food for those who want to lose weight.

ROOT VEGETABLES

Traditionally, vegetables were chiefly represented by such root vegetables as daikon radishes, carrots, and burdock, which are rich in dietary fiber, so few people died of colon or rectal cancer. However, recently the number of people who develop cancer has been increasing. Therefore, we should eat more root vegetables to prevent constipation, obesity, and cancer.

DAIKON

(Japanese white radish)

For prevention of colon cancer

Daikon has a substance, which promotes the secretion of gastric juice, aids digestion, and puts bowel movement in order.

It is also a good source of vitamin C, which relives fatigue, and dietary fiber, which prevents colon cancer. Its green tops are edible and contains plenty of calcium, iron and vitamins A and C.

Effective for
Aiding digestion
Relieving fatigue
Preventing sunburn

Always have on hand for a good appetite and digestion

Spicy Daikon Pickles

Ingredients: 3 inches (8 cm) daikon / ½ carrot / 1 Tbsp dried shrimp / ⅓ scallion / 1 clove ginger / 2 tsps Japanese pepper seeds / dash salt / sauce (2 Tbsps soy sauce / 1 Tbsp vinegar / 1 Tbsp sesame oil / ½ tsp sugar)

Method: **1.** Dice daikon into ⅜ inch (1 cm) thick cubes and carrot into ¼ inch (¾ cm) thick cubes. Sprinkle with salt and set aside for 20 minutes. Wash in water and drain.

2. Mince scallion and ginger finely.

3. Combine sauce ingredients in a bowl. Add daikon, carrot, dried shrimp, pepper seeds, long onion and ginger and mix well.

4. Let stand for 30 minutes until well seasoned.

*It can be stored with the sauce in the refrigerator for about 1 week.

Tasty daikon for a cold day

Korean-style Braised Daikon

Ingredients: ½ daikon (1¾ lbs or 800 g) / 7 oz (200 g) chopped beef / ½ leek / 1 clove garlic / 2 tsps soy sauce / 2 tsps sesame oil / 1 tsp toasted white sesame seeds / 2 red chili peppers / 1 Tbsp salad oil / broth (½ cup water / 2½ Tbsps each of mirin, sake and soy sauce)

Method: **1.** Chop daikon in chunks.

2. Shred leek and garlic. Combine with soy sauce, sesame oil and toasted sesame seeds.

3. Mix beef with (2) and set aside.

4. Heat salad oil in a pan. Sauté beef until color changes. Add daikon, seeded red chili pepper and fry for another minute. Pour broth over all.

5. Cover with a lid and simmer over medium heat until daikon becomes soft for 20 to 25 minutes.

For Colds and Sore Throats

When you are coming down with a cold, drink this syrup. It will stifle the cough and relieve the sore throat. This is because vitamin C and other substances contained in daikon permeate into the syrup.

Daikon in Syrup

Ingredients and method: **1.** Wash 14 oz (400 g) daikon in water and drain. Cut into ⅛ inch (5 mm) thick slices.

2. Put daikon in a preserving jar. Add 4 Tbsps corn syrup or honey. Cover and let stand for 2 or 3 days.

3. When the daikon becomes soft, drink the syrup. The daikon can also be eaten.

TURNIP

Relieve stomachaches

Effective for
Aiding digestion
Relieving fatigue
Stifling coughs

Like daikon, turnips have digestive enzymes such as diastase and vitamin C. In Chinese medicine, it is said to activate internal organs and relieve stomachaches. It has also been used to supress coughs and treat chilblains, and chapped skin.

Make tasty by seasoning with kombu

Turnip Mixed with Kombu Kelp

When kombu is salty, use a small quantity.

Ingredients: 2 turnips / leaves of 2 turnips / ⅔ oz (20 g) salted kombu / dash salt

Method: 1. Peel turnips and quarter. Cut into thin round slices.

2. Cut leaves into ⅜ inch (1 cm) lengths.

3. Rub (1) and (2) with salt until tender. Wash in water and drain.

4. Mix (3) with kombu and let stand for 1 to 2 hours so that turnips are seasoned with kombu.

For warming the body and good for the stomach

Turnip with Sea Bass

Ingredients: 1 or 2 turnips (1¾ lbs or 800 g) / 18 oz (500 g) bony parts of sea bass / dash salt / broth《¾ cup kombu-dashi (kelp soup) / 4 Tbsps sake / 1 Tbsp mirin (sweet sake) / 3 Tbsps soy sauce》 / kinome (leaf buds of Japanese pepper)

Method: 1. Salt bony parts of sea bass lightly. Scald in boiling water followed by a bath of cold water. Scale and remove stains and place on a bamboo basket.

2. Peel turnip and cut into halves.

3. Bring broth to a boil in a pan. Add turnips and (1). Simmer over medium heat until turnips become soft.

4. Serve in a bowl topping with kinome.

＊Shredded peel of yuzu (Japanese citrus fruit) can be substituted for kinome.

TARO

Chinese-style Mashed Taro

A digestive enzyme, mucin, is contained in the sticky part, and it aids digestion and moves the bowels.

Effective for
- Aiding digestion
- Relieving constipation
- Intestinal regulation

Ingredients: 8 taro (10½ oz or 300 g) / ½ clove ginger / dash vinegar / 1 Tbsp sesame oil / 2 Tbsps each of soy sauce and mirin / leek or scallion

Method: 1. Pare taro and wash in water. Boil in salted and vinegared water for 7 to 8 minutes and wash quickly.

2. Mash hot taro with a fork or masher. Combine grated ginger, sesame oil, soy sauce, mirin and dash salt and mix well.

3. Place on a plate and sprinkle with chopped long onion.

* Instead of boiling taro, you may wrap it in a plastic food wrap and cook in a microwave oven for 5 to 6 minutes.

YAM

Chinese yam

Japanese yam

Grated Yam Topping

The yam contains vitamin C as well as starch. It also has plenty of digestive enzyme, amylase, which decomposes starch.

Effective for
- Toning the body
- Aiding digestion
- Intestinal regulation

Ingredients: 7oz(200g) yam / 7 oz (200 g) raw tuna / 1 Tbsp soy sauce / dash vinegar / aonori (toasted and powdered green laver) / grated horseradish

Method: 1. Dice tuna in ½ inch (1.5 cm) cubes and season with soy sauce.

2. Pare yams, soak in vinegared water for a short time and grate.

3. Put tuna in a bowl and pour yams over them. Sprinkle with aonori and serve with grated horseradish.

* Yams can be eaten raw when grated. You may cut them and mash with a wooden pestle to make digestive enzymes effective.

For Increasing Body Tone

Rice Gruel with Yam and Walnut

Ingredients and method: 1. Put ½ cup washed rice and 2½ cups water in a thick pan and set aside for over 30 minutes.

2. Add 3 oz (85 g) sanyaku (dried yam) and cook over medium heat. When it comes to a boil, stir the whole with a wooden spatula. Reduce the heat and move the cover of the pan a little to avoid over boiling. Simmer for about 50 minutes.

3. Turn off heat and allow cooked rice to settle for 5 minutes. Sprinkle with salt and 8 chopped walnuts.

* Sanyaku (dried yam) is available at Chinese medicine drugstores.

SWEET POTATO

Twice as much dietary fiber as potatoes / For relieving constipation

Effective for

Beautiful skin

Preventing colds

Intestinal regulation

Sweet potatoes have a good deal of dietary fiber. The content of vitamin C is 30 mg in 100 g, and it is resistant to heat. The yellow-colored ones are a good source of vitamins A and B_1. They are particularly effective for making skin beautiful. In Chinese medicine, they have been used to make the stomach strong and increase vitality.

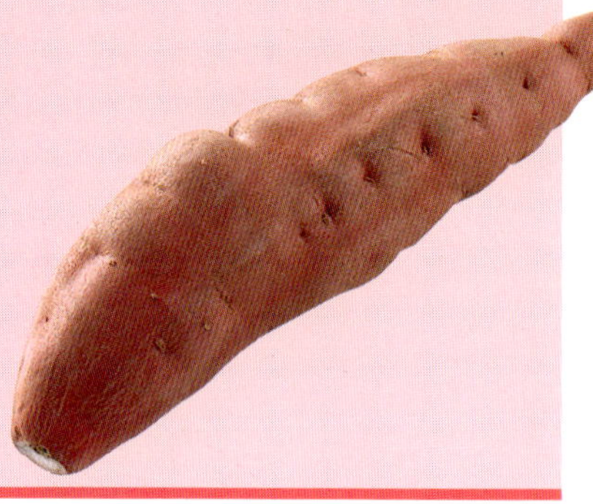

Vitamin C increased by adding green tea

Deep-fried Sweet Potato

Ingredients: 1 sweet potato (14 oz or 400 g) / 1 Tbsp powdered green tea / oil for deep-frying

Method: 1. Wash sweet potato well in water and cut into 2 inch (5 cm) sticks. Soak in water.

2. Pat dry and deep-fry in oil at 340°F (170°C) for about 2 minutes.

3. When cooked, drain and sprinkle with powdered green tea.

Flavored by fruit

Sweet Potato Layers

Ingredients: 1 sweet potato (10½ oz or 300 g) / 1 apple / ⅓ cup raisins / 3 Tbsps sugar / 3 Tbsps butter / dash salt and cinnamon

Method: 1. Wash sweet potato well and cut into ⅜ inch (1 cm) thick slices with skin. Pare apple and cut in quarters and slice.

2. Butter a pan and place ⅓ each of ingredients; sweet potato, apple, raisin, sugar and butter in this order (photo below). Repeat the same 3 times and sprinkle with salt and cinnamon. Add ½ cup water.

3. Cover with a paper lid and boil down over medium heat for about 30 minutes until the liquid is almost evaporated.

POTATO

Plenty of vitamin C protects the stomach from ulcers

Potatoes are a valuable source of vitamin C in the northern countries. Like the vitamin C of sweet potatoes, it is resistant to heat and well preserved without damage. They are effective for strenghtening the mucous membrane of the stomach, promoting the discharge of salt and bringing down the blood pressure. They are also recommended to relieve constipation.

Effective for
- **Preventing stomach ulcers**
- **Preventing hypertension**
- **Relieving constipation**

Simple and easy cooking

Curried Potato Salad

Ingredients: 12 small potatoes / dash salt / ½ tsp curry powder / 1 Tbsp salad oil / dressing (½ tsp curry powder / 1 Tbsp vinegar / 2 Tbsps salad oil / dash salt and pepper) / Italian parsley

Method: 1. Wash potatoes, rubbing the skin in water. Coat with salt, curry powder, and salad oil thoroughly.

2. Wrap in a aluminum foil and bake in an oven (400°F/200°C) for about 30 minutes.

3. Combine the ingredients of dressing well and pour over hot potatoes.

4. Garnish with Italian parsley.

With three kinds of vegetables

Potato Cooked with Tomato

Ingredients: 4 small potatoes / 1 onion / 2 tomatoes / 3 Tbsps butter / ½ bouillon cube / salt and pepper / chopped parsley

Method: 1. Cut potatoes into ⅜ inch (1 cm) thick slices and soak in water.

2. Cut onion into slices. Blanch tomatoes and discard stalk ends and seeds and dice into ⅜ inch (1 cm) cubes.

3. Butter a pan lightly. Place ⅓ each of potatoes, onion, tomatoes and butter in this order and sprinkle with salt and pepper. Repeat the same 3 times.

4. Add ½ water and crushed bouillon cube and cover with a paper lid. Simmer for about 40 minutes over medium heat. Sprinkle with parsley.

LOTUS ROOT

Good for nursing a hangover

Effective for

Intestinal regulation

Relieving coughs

Stopping bleeding

A hundred grams of lotus root contains 55 mg of vitamin C. It also has a good deal of dietary fiber and regulates the intestines. In Chinese medicine, they are used to stifle coughs, relieve asthma, and stop bleeding. In China, the whole lotus is made use of as medicine, from the root, stalk, leaf, flower, fruit and bud.

Grated Lotus Root Soup

Ingredients: 7 oz (200 g) lotus root / 4 cups dashi soup (see inside front cover) / 1 Tbsp sake / 1 tsp salt / 1 tsp soy sauce / 1 umeboshi (pickled plum) / vinegar

Method: 1. Pare lotus root and soak in vinegared water.

2. Pat dry and grate. Add dashi soup and put all in a pan. Simmer for 7 to 8 minutes.

3. Season with sake, salt and soy sauce. Serve in a bowl with a seeded umeboshi put on top.

Deep-fried Lotus Root Sandwich

Ingredients: 12 oz (340 g) lotus root / 7 oz (200 g) ground pork / ½ leek / juice of 1 clove ginger / 1 tsp soy sauce / 1 tsp sake / 2 tsps cornstarch / oil for deep-frying

Method: 1. Pare lotus root and cut into 16 round slices. Chop leek finely.

2. Combine ground pork, leek, ginger juice, soy sauce, sake and cornstarch in a bowl and mix well. Divide into 8.

3. Coat lotus root with flour. Sandwich (2) with lotus root as shown in the photo. Deep-fry in oil heated to 340°F/170°C for 5 to 6 minutes.

For a hangover

For relieving constipation

BURDOCK ROOT

For cleaning the intestines

Mostly made of fibrous elements, the burdock root contains cellulose, which is insoluble in water, and lignin, which is said to prevent colon cancer. These substances are indigestible, so they clean the intestines and move the bowels. Moreover, they reduce blood cholesterol and prevent hardening of the arteries.

Effective for

Relieving constipation

Preventing arteriosclerosis

Preventing colon cancer

Burdock Root Salad

Ingredients: 1 small burdock root (10½ oz or 300 g) / 1¾ oz (50 g) carrot / dressing (2 Tbsps salad oil / 1 Tbsp vinegar / 1 Tbsp soy sauce / dash powdered chili pepper or paprika) / 4 shiso (perilla) leaves / vinegar

Method: **1.** Scrub skins off burdock root with the back of a knife. Peel carrot and cut into 1½ inches (4 cm) length strips.

2. Boil carrot for 30 seconds in water. Boil burdock root in vinegared water for 1 minute. Drain and let cool.

3. Combine the ingredients of dressing and mix with (2). Top with shredded shiso leaves.

Burdock Root Wrapped in Beef

Ingredients: 4 new (slender) burdock roots / 12 oz (340 g) beef slices / seasoning (1 Tbsp soy sauce / 1 Tbsp sake) / cornstarch / vinegar / oil for deep-frying / flowers of wasabi horseradish

Method: **1.** Scrub skins off burdock roots and cut into 1½ inches (4 cm) length sticks. Boil in vinegared water for about 3 minutes.

2. Season beef with soy sauce and sake.

3. Wrap 4 to 5 burdock root sticks in beef as shown in the photo. Dredge with cornstarch.

4. Deep-fry in oil at 340°F/170°C for 3 minutes and remove to a plate. Garnish with flowers of wasabi horseradish. Serve with powdered sansho (Japanese pepper seeds) mixed with salt.

Burdock root wrapped in beef

Crispy and tasty healthful food

HEALTHFUL

Broths made from root vegetable
healthful food. Our editorial staf
ularity and their nutrition an
follows.

Four kinds of vegetables

Made with just four ingredients: carrot, daikon, daikon leaves, burdock root and dried shiitake mushroom. The carrot, daikon and burdock root are cooked without paring their skins to make the most of their nutrients. Use shiitake which was dried in the sun.

The nutrients in the vegetables

The four vegetables listed above are very nutritious. Carrot is rich in beta carotene (converted to vitamin A in the body), which has antioxidant properties that may protect against cancer. It also contains sulfur and minerals like phosphorus and calcium.

Daikon has several kinds of digestive enzymes such as diastase and a good deal of vitamin C. It also contains dietary fiber, lignin, which is said to be effective for preventing colon cancer. Daikon leaves are a good source of calcium, which builds strong bones and prevents osteoporosis; iron, which is indispensable for the prevention of anemia; and vitamins A and C.

Similar to the daikon, the burdock root has lignin and plenty of dietary fiber like cellulose.

The dried shiitake mushroom (exposed to the sun) is rich in vitamin D, which promotes the absorption of calcium and helps development of bones. Of course, it contains a good deal of dietary fiber, which includes an anti-cancer substance.

Vegetable Broth

Ingredients for 1 serving:
½ carrot / ¼ daikon / ¼ daikon leaves / ¼ thick burdock root / 1 sun-dried shiitake mushroom

*The broth can be kept in a glass container and stored in the refrigerator. But it easily spoils, so it can not be preserved long. Drink it up in one or two days.

Method:1. Wash carrot, daikon, daikon leaves and burdock root well in water. Cut all unpared in large chunks. Use mushroom with its stem.

2. Place all the ingredients in a pan. Pour in about 10 cups (3 times the amount of the ingredients) of water and boil over high heat.

3. When it comes to a boil, turn heat low and simmer for about 1 hour. Let it cool. When cooled keep in a preserving jar.

VEGETABLE BROTH

have historically been valued as a
probed into the secret of their pop-
effect, and summarized them as

Minerals are contained in broths

What kinds of nutrients are dissolved into vegetable broths? From the carrot, such minerals as sulfur, selenium and part of beta carotene are dissolved in the broth. From the daikon and daikon leaves, vitamin C, which is soluble in water; and such minerals as zinc, iron, and phosphorus are dissolved. However, fat-soluble vitamins like vitamins A and E, and dietary fiber contained in the burdock root and other vegetables are not soluble in the broth. Vitamins, which absorb water, seem to be effective for relieving constipation. Generally speaking, it can be said that broths contain minerals and vitamin C.

The vegetables which remain are edible

After the broth is cooked plenty of nutrients remain in the vegetables. The dietary fiber is indispensable for preventing constipation and adult diseases like arteriosclerosis and hypertension. Vitamin A, which prevents colds and relieves eye strain, vitamin E, which slows the aging process of blood vessels, and almost all of the vitamin D still remains in the vegetables. Although some vitamins and enzymes are destroyed by heat, you should eat the remaining vegetables. However, they are not tasty to eat owing to their alkaline flavor. Therefore you might fry them in oil and season them. They might also be used in hotchpotch or in miso soup. Another way is to cook them together with meat or fish. But be careful not to eat too much of them, because intaking a large quantity of alkalinity is harmful.

SEA VEGETABLES

Called sea vegetables, seaweed is high in fiber and rich in iodine. Insufficient intake of iodine causes diseases such as goiter, but Japanese people have no fear of the shortage since they are surrounded by the sea. The dietary fiber contained in the seaweed is soluble in water, so it does not fill the stomach.

KOMBU KELP

Rich in iodine, and prevents goiter

dried shredded kombu

The nutrients of kombu kelp, which is used for a flavorful broth and cooked with other ingredients, are rich in variety. It is a good source of iodine, which prevents goiter; calcium; vitamin A and dietary fiber. It also contains a substance, which brings down the blood pressure.

Effective for
- Preventing obesity
- Preventing hypertension
- Relieving constipation

For preventing constipation

Sweet Potato Cooked with Kombu Kelp

Ingredients: 1⅖ oz (40 g) dried shredded kombu kelp / 1 sweet potato / broth (½ cup water / 2 tsps sugar / 2 tsps soy sauce / dash salt)

Method: 1. Soak kombu in water to remove sand and change water. Soak again.

2. Wash sweet potato in water. Cut diagonally with skin and soak in water.

3. Put (1), (2) in a pan and cover with water. Cook for about 10 minutes.

4. Season with sugar, soy sauce and salt. Simmer over low heat until the liquid is evaporated.

∗Let kombu and sweet potato absorb broth thoroughly.

WAKAME

Iodine produces a hormone which activates metabolism

Wakame is familiar to Japanese people. It is rich in iodine and calcium, so it is highly recommended to growing children and pregnant women. It also contains water-soluble fiber, which is good for the stomach, and alginic acid.

Effective for
- Preventing hypertension
- Preventing osteoporosis
- Preventing arteriosclerosis

Oil helps absorption of iodine

Stir-fried Wakame

Ingredients: 4⅕ oz (120 g) salted wakame / 1 tsp soy sauce / 2 tsps toasted white sesame seeds / dash powdered red chili pepper / 1½ Tbsps salad oil

Method: 1. Cut wakame into bite-sized pieces. Wash and drain.

2. Heat oil in a pan and stir-fry wakame. Season with soy sauce.

3. Place the wakame on a plate. Sprinkle with sesame seeds and powdered red chili pepper.

∗Salted wakame should be washed well in water to remove salt. When using dried wakame, ⅛ oz (4 g) per person should be soaked in water. If you pour hot water over it, the color will turn bright.

Acid taste stimulates the appetite

Vinegared Vegetables with Wakame

Ingredients: 1 stalk celery / 2 large cabbage leaves / wakame vinegar《⅓ oz (10 g) ita (dried) wakame / 1½ Tbsps vinegar / 1½ Tbsps sesame oil / ⅓ Tbsp soy sauce》/ dash salt

Method: 1. Remove the outer ribs of celery and core of cabbage. Shred all and soak in salted water until tender. Press lightly to remove excess water.

2. Toast dried wakame and wrap in cloth and crush with hands. Combine vinegar, sesame oil and soy sauce.

3. Mix in celery and cabbage.

∗ When ita wakame is unavailable, chopped salted wakame may be substituted.

Effective for
Preventing hypertension
Preventing osteoporosis
Preventing anemia

HIJIKI
(A kind of brown algae)

Hijiki is a good source of dietary fiber, vitamins A and D, and calcium. If cooked with oil, the rate of absorption of vitamins A and D increases.

Korean-style Hijiki with Beef

Ingredients: 2 oz (60 g) hijiki / 7 oz (200 g) beef slices / ½ clove ginger / 1½ inch (4 cm) leek / broth 《2 Tbsps soy sauce / 1 Tbsp sake / pinch sugar / ½ cup dashi soup (see inside front cover)》/ 1 Tbsp toasted white sesame seeds / dash powdered red chili pepper / 1 Tbsp salad oil

Method: **1.** Soak hijiki in water and drain. Cut long hijiki in bite-sized lengths.
2. Cut beef in strips and shred ginger and leek.
3. Heat oil in a pan and stir-fry (2). Add hijiki and stir-fry.
4. When fried thoroughly, pour broth over all. Simmer over medium heat for about 15 minutes. Sprinkle with chopped sesame seeds and powdered red chili pepper.

Effective for
Preventing constipation
Preventing obesity
Preventing arteriosclerosis

NORI LAVER

A good source of vitamins A, B_1, B_2, and C, calcium, iron, and dietary fiber. It is said that the chlorophyll contained in the nori laver reduces blood cholesterol.

Nori Laver Soup

Ingredients: 4 sheets nori laver / ½ clove ginger / broth 《3 cups dashi soup (see inside front cover) / 2 tsps sake / 1 tsp soy sauce / ½ tsp salt / 1 tsp sesame oil》

Method: **1.** Toast nori and crush with hands. Shred ginger.
2. In dashi soup add sake, soy sauce, salt and sesame oil and bring to a boil.
3. Put (1) in a serving bowl and cover with the hot broth.

Cook Seaweed with Oil

There are about 60 kinds of edible seaweed. They are classified into four types; green, brown, red, and blue-green algae. These algae photosynthesize and produce starch, pigments and other organic substances. Seaweed has no calories and produces no energy. That is because the indigestible dietary fiber passes through the intestines. Most of the fiber is alginic acid, which is soluble in water and soothes the stomach. The fiber contained in mushrooms and other vegetables is water-insoluble, so they fill the stomach. Accordingly, you should eat both of

MOZUKU

(An algae-like seaweed)

Rich in dietary fiber. Vinegared mozuku has a tasty, sticky texture. Rice porridge with a large quantity of mozuku is worth trying.

Effective for
Preventing constipation
Preventing obesity
Preventing arteriosclerosis

Vinegared Mozuku with Grated Yam

Ingredients: 1⅖ oz (40 g) mozuku / 4⅕ oz (120 g) yam / dash vinegar / vinegar mixture 《2 Tbsps vinegar / 2 tsps sugar / 1 Tbsp happo dashi (see inside front cover)》

Method: 1. Put mozuku in a bamboo basket and wash under running water and drain. Pare yam and soak in vinegared water for a while. Drain and grate.

2. Put mozuku and yam in a bowl and pour vinegar mixture over them.

＊The combination of mozuku and yam has traditionally been appreciated. The sticky and soft texture will especially be favored by aged people.

AGAR-AGAR

Japanese agar-agar, called 'kanten,' is a gel made from seaweed. The content of dietary fiber is the highest of all foods. It is used in the preparation of salads and gelatine-like puddings.

Effective for
Preventing constipation
Preventing obesity
Preventing arteriosclerosis

Three-colored Agar-agar Salad

Ingredients: ⅓ oz (10 g) itokanten (string agar-agar) / ½ udo (5¼ oz or 150 g) / 1 cucumber / 3 oz (85 g) carrot / ½ clove ginger / dash salt / dressing (1 Tbsp vinegar / 2 Tbsps soy sauce / 1 Tbsp sesame oil)

Method: 1. Soak itokanten in water and cut into bite-sized length.

2. Shred cucumber and carrot in 1½ inch (4 cm) strips and rub with salt. Wash in water and squeeze out water. Shred ginger and udo and soak in water.

3. Place (1) and (2) on a plate as shown in the photo. Top with ginger and pour dressing over all.

them.

Seaweed is a good source of vitamins A, B_1, B_2, C, calcium and iron. However, it is an indigestible food and poor in absorption. Since vitamin A is soluble in oil, you should make use of oil in the preparation or cook it with fried-tofu. By using oil, the rate of absorption increases, and it becomes tasty. It also helps absorption of minerals.

The iodine contained in the seaweed produces thyroid hormone, which is related to metabolism. The shortage of the hormone causes obesity, and makes it difficult to warm the body. In some countries in the desert, people are required to take salt that contains iodine.

List of Effective Vegetables